Dedication

To my amazing clients.
You inspire me every day with what you achieve,
and how you live your lives.

Contents

Introduction	1
Chapter 1: Unlocking Your Brain to Create the Most Amazing, Crazy and Uplifting Life	3
Chapter 2: Are You Living Your Life on Autopilot?	15
Chapter 3: Using Regret as Your Rocket Fuel	25
Chapter 4: Brain Basics and How You Create Your World	35
Chapter 5: The Child at the Wheel: Navigating Adult Life with Childhood Maps	51
Chapter 6: Drop Your Crap	65
Chapter 7: Peeling Back the Layers of You	77
Chapter 8: Meet the Real You	95
Chapter 9: Vision Creates Clarity	109
Chapter 10: Expand your Possibilities	121
Chapter 11: Transforming Lives With Lollipops	131
Chapter 12: Let's Play	139
Chapter 13: Your Life Transformed	145
References & Resources	151
About the Author	153

Introduction

Hello my dear reader.

It's truly wonderful to meet you.

Something has drawn you to this book, and to open it at this very moment. Maybe it was the title. Maybe it was something on the cover that sparked your interest. Maybe it was something else… something subtle yet powerful, or something completely and almost random.

Whatever it was that called you to have this book, and then propelled you to open it to the first page where you are right now, I want you to take that as a sign. A sign that something inside you is ready for change.

- Perhaps it's a desire for growth, a longing for transformation, or a journey for deeper understanding.
- It could be the need to break free from the monotony of daily routines, or an urge to discover new parts of yourself.
- Maybe you're seeking answers to questions that have lingered at the back of your mind, or you're looking for inspiration to ignite your passions.

Ultimate Brain Hacks

Whatever your reason, acknowledge that you have taken the first step towards something new.

And that step is significant.

You've chosen to acquire this book, in whichever way best suits you, and to open its pages to read. This is not just a random act at an inconsequential time; it's a deliberate choice, a step forward within your right timing towards a future that holds more promise, more fulfilment.

This book isn't about vague promises or theoretical possibilities, or heavy science. It aims to inspire you, to help you understand, and to give you real, tangible results. This book is more than just words on a page – it's an interactive experience.

At the end of each chapter, you'll find a 'Brain Hack' for you to work through, designed to help you create new neuronal pathways, gain fresh insights, and, ultimately, transform your world. By completing the exercises in this book, you'll gain insights that can transform your understanding of yourself and others.

My goal with writing this book is to unlock the hidden barriers within your mind, to inspire and empower you to create the life you desire. This journey isn't just about reading; it's about doing, feeling, and ultimately, becoming the person you've always known you could be.

So, take a deep breath, open your heart, and prepare to embark on a transformative journey within yourself.

CHAPTER 1

Unlocking Your Brain to Create the Most Amazing, Crazy and Uplifting Life

Introducing the Awakened

Having studied the intricacies of the brain and witnessed the 'transformation' of many people over the years, I have realised that there are two types of people. There are the 'passengers', those you see riding the conveyor belt of their life, and then there are the 'awakened,' those who exude something different. Something almost magical.

Ultimate Brain Hacks

Looking on the surface, you may not be able to tell them apart. Both could be moving through life gathering the typical trophies: completing school, pursuing further studies, landing that job, finding a partner, getting married, buying a first house, having children, and so forth. In the workplace, they might be climbing the corporate ladder or, as business owners, seemingly grinding day in and day out.

But look deeper, and this is where it gets interesting. The passengers are on a conveyor belt. Deep down, something doesn't sit well with them — they yearn for something more fulfilling.

Passengers are all around you:

- In the supermarket line - lost in thought, mechanically going through the motions, their eyes often glazed over as they wait their turn.
- In cafes - sitting with their coffee, their eyes distant, not truly present, scrolling through their phones or staring blankly out the window.
- Walking along the street - yes, their bodies may be there, but they seem like empty shells, cycling through the motions of life.

There's an emptiness or numbness in passengers. A lack of sparkle and magic as they navigate their daily routines. Many are 'happy enough', but they do not realise that they are on the conveyor belt.

In contrast, the awakened are those who have stepped off the societal conveyor belt and live their lives with richness and fullness. They are active captains of their lives, navigating every moment with passion, power, purpose, and joy. There is a distinct sparkle in their eyes, an unmistakable glow that sets them apart. When you meet them, there's an almost magical quality to them. They seem to attract opportunities and positive experiences effortlessly.

The awakened have a magnetic presence. They draw people in with their enthusiasm, energy and zest for life. Their excitement is infectious, and their positivity radiates outwards. They have lived amazing, incredible and sometimes crazy lives. They inspire others around them. Things just happen for them, almost as if by magic.

The awakened believe in the possibility of change—change for themselves, change in their lives, and change for humankind. They live each day with intentionality, seeking out experiences and opportunities that align with their true desires and values.

The awakened are few and far between. They can be difficult to find, but once you encounter one, you cannot forget them. Their impact is profound, leaving a lasting impression on those they meet.

Who Are You?

So, what do you have to do to become one of the awakened? Spend a moment on each of the following questions and see what comes up for you.

- Who are you?
- Are you living in the richness and fullness of your life?
- Are you on the societal conveyor belt of life, or are you a captain in your life?
- If you've answered that you are a captain in your life, how do you know?

Ultimate Brain Hacks

Your answers to these questions could represent 'an itch', or a lingering thought that you've had for quite a while. A thought that you haven't wanted to face, or an itch that you haven't quite been able to scratch. It may have been persisting on and off for years.

Or you might be at some form of a crossroads in your life — be it career, relationship, health, love, family, or happiness.

Perhaps you're wanting the confidence to make the right choice, or clarity and direction. You may even have been stuck at this fork for quite some time… weeks, years, even decades. Yet something always stands in the way, be it fear, lack of confidence, paralysis, or self-sabotage.

Perhaps you're grappling with habits you long to break, but just never seem to. These habits could be procrastination or unhealthy lifestyle choices or negative thinking patterns and unproductive routines.

Or you've reached an uneasy professional comfortableness. Potentially one with golden handcuffs, limiting where you can go or what you can do. You might feel secure in your job, but there's a nagging sense that you're not living up to your full potential, that there's something more out there waiting for you.

If you are feeling a little down right now, that's okay. You are exactly where you need to be to start your journey of awakening.

Creating That Sparkle in Your Life

Let's now focus on creating the sparkle, and magic that could be in your life. Sit for a moment and answer the following questions.

- What would 'sparkle' in your life look like to you?
- What would being 'awakened' look like to you?
- How would it look if you lived a life of amazingness?

You may not have the answers to the questions above. But how would you feel if you did?

Imagine that you had all the answers right in front of you with a tool of unparalleled potential, to create the most amazing, fantastic and unbelievable life. A life worth living. And this tool that has the power to radically transform every aspect of your existence— your relationships, career, health, the very essence of your being.

Sounds impossible right?

Not so.

This is not the realm of science fiction or fantasy, or even AI. It is the reality of the complex, enigmatic organ that resides right within your skull. This is your brain, with unlimited potential to adapt, learn, and evolve. Your brain stands at the core of every dream you dare to dream and every challenge you face.

By delving into the inner workings of your brain, you can navigate your thoughts and emotions with greater mastery and create absolute magic in your life.

You have the choice to live a super-amazing, fabulous, fun and fulfilled life. This is a big claim, but I truly believe that your own transformation lies within these very pages, and the questions that you will answer.

- Are you ready to start on this journey to see how the principles of neuroscience can shed light on your own path to sparkle?
- Are you ready to create a life of more?
- A life of pure bliss?
- A life without regret?
- A life of magic?

As we move forward, remember that this exploration of your brain, brain hacks and your life is not just about self-improvement—it's about reimagining you and your place in the world.

LET'S BRAIN HACK: SETTING YOUR INTENTION

Whenever we go into situations, the best outcomes occur when we set our intention for it.

So, whatever your situation is right now as you read this book, I want you to take a moment to pause and set your intention for this book. This may be difficult for you to answer, from such a simple question. But I want you to spend a moment now, thinking about what you want to achieve by working through this book. This may seem like a sudden thing to do, but often we instinctively know. The first thing that comes to mind when you read the question should be your answer. It is now time to set your intention: what would you like to have achieved once you've turned the last page?

_____

_____

_____

If you've just skipped this exercise, I want you to go back again and complete it. Answer in the space above - What is your intention for reading this book?

Before you finish this chapter. Sit for a moment and ponder what you'd like to achieve by using this book. Really open your mind. If you are having trouble articulating it, here are some examples:

- It could be defining what your best life looks like and taking the steps towards it.
- It could be gathering new insights on yourself
- It could be to change a habit.
- It could be to understand the brain better.

If you are still feeling resistance to doing this intention setting exercise, ask yourself *'why?'* Is there a block there? What is stopping you from answering? Write out your block below (Yes – writing out your blockages is another brain hack exercise):

_____

_____

_____

_____

To set your intention when reading a book may seem trivial at first, but let's expand this concept further. Imagine setting your intention at the start of a meeting, or even at the beginning of your day, week, month, or year.

When you broaden the scope of intention-setting, it becomes a powerful tool.

Setting your intention is a simple yet profound brain hack that can direct your focus, shape your actions, and ultimately transform your life. This practice, though easy to implement, yields significant dividends in clarity, purpose, and fulfilment.

Let's now spend a moment talking about brain hacks. Each brain hack has been designed to engage your mind in ways that promote growth, creativity, and assist you to take the wheel for your life. Working through each brain hack offers more than just an opportunity to learn something new; it is a step toward unlocking your mind and rewiring your brain for greater.

If you choose to participate actively in these exercises, you will experience profound changes in your life and your well-being. This can influence all aspects of your life.

Conversely, not completing the brain hacks can mean that you are missing out on the life changing opportunities that this book presents. While it's comfortable to remain within the bounds of familiar habits, non-participation in these hacks will result in nothing changing. And over time, the gap widens between those who participate, and those who don't. This isn't just about losing out on minor improvements; it's about forgoing the chance to achieve a significantly more amazing and sparkly life.

By choosing to engage with these brain hacks, you're not just completing a task — you're investing in yourself. While some of the brain hacks may seem incredibly simple, don't underestimate the effect. They are here to provide insight, to plant a seed, ready for the next one. Like the concept of 'compounding interest' that we were taught at school, the compounding effect of those that participate in these brain hacks can be the difference between a super amazing life, or merely surviving.

So, take a deep breath. You've got this. It's time to brain hack and set your intention; What would you like to achieve by working through this book?

_____

_____

_____

_____

Wow. Well done. Congratulations on taking action and starting that process of compounding action in your life.

Let's move forward now to unlock the secrets of your brain and lead a more fulfilling, aligned, passionate, empowered, and purposeful life.

Key Highlights on how to create your most crazy, amazing, uplifting life

Are you a passenger in your life or living a life of an awakened? Passengers move through life on autopilot, while the awakened have a magnetic presence, a distinct sparkle in their eyes, and the ability to attract positive experiences effortlessly.

You have everything you need right here to become awakened. By delving into the inner workings of your brain, you can navigate your thoughts, emotions, worlds, and create magic in your life.

Set your intention for reading this book. Do the brain hacks that are set! NOTE: if you have skipped to this part, go back and set your intention.

CHAPTER 2

Are You Living Your Life on Autopilot?

I want you to imagine a typical day for you right now. Perhaps you leap out of bed, energised, maybe squeeze in some exercise, before chaos reigns. Or perhaps you roll out of bed and grab your toast and coffee. Then, the whirlwind starts. You prep for work, pack lunches for you, the kids, start work, juggle endless meetings, client appointments, tasks, and deadlines.

After work, it's a sprint through homework, kids' sports, dinner, and bedtime routines until you collapse, exhausted, craving a moment just for yourself. You may or may not get that moment.

Ultimate Brain Hacks

There's just… no time. No time to think. No time to feel. No time to understand you. Who you are and what you want.

Each day, you follow a script that's become so familiar, you hardly need to think about what comes next. As we grow through life, it is easy to slip into routines, into repetitive behaviours, into comfortable habits. Days slip by… and merge into weeks… and weeks into years… For reasons that you may not even remember now, you've sought comfort, familiarity and routine. With intent, or without…it's just happened over time. And as you live in the monotony of your life, over time you've lost the spark that was uniquely you.

Spend a moment thinking about when was the last time that you felt truly connected to yourself. As in, truly alive and excited to be you, your unique you and excited for the day, and your life ahead.

Perhaps you never had that spark, you've never known the 'real you'. You're not even sure what I'm talking about. You have never had that experience. You'd like to know what that looks like. It's an uncomfortable thought. One that we don't like to delve on for long.

What happens with these uncomfortable, searching thoughts are that often, there comes a pivotal moment - perhaps monumental, or perhaps subtle, that forces you to reflect on you and your path to now.

This moment of insight could strike with the suddenness of a thunderclap in your life – an unexpected diagnosis, the sudden loss of someone close, or a career upheaval. Or it could arrive more gradually, marked by life transitions such as a long-term relationship ending, or watching your children leave the home to forge their paths.

Are You Living Your Life on Autopilot?

Perhaps this moment is now, as you turn these pages.

Maybe it's that whisper that has lingered in the back of your mind, often overlooked yet persistent. Now, it speaks with an urgency that cannot be ignored, nudging you to acknowledge that there is more to your life, more depth and fulfilment possible than where you are now.

Questions that you might've asked yourself, like:

- Who am I?
- Who am I, truly?
- Am I truly happy?
- Have I ever been truly happy?
- What has happened to my life?
- How have I got myself to this point?

Feeling uncomfortable yet? Good. That discomfort is your sign of awakening.

Are You Ready to Change Now?

Our brains like the feeling of comfort, safety and predictability. We will naturally choose activities, routines, and the ease of knowing what is next, over the unknown.

We fear change. Change can be daunting. Change carries the risk of pain. We worry in change. We worry about what lies ahead. We worry about the unknown. This fear can be paralysing, causing us to cling to the familiar, the old, even when it no longer serves us. And often, we do not even acknowledge the fear.

Countless people today are trapped in the relentless rhythm of the same routine, year after year, all held back by the fear of the unknown. Even thinking about a change can often bring us the full mind relay loop that can overwhelm us. For example:

- What if the decision to change careers leads to failure?
- What if ending a comfortable, but stagnant relationship brings loneliness?
- What if moving to a new city doesn't solve the problems we're trying to escape?
- What if we exercise, and we are judged, or even worse, we hurt ourselves?

We often get so caught in our looping thoughts, that we don't make that change. We don't take a step in a different direction.

A single step towards change is accepting that change means that life will be different. But different is ok.

Different can be even good for us. Different can also be the gateway to new possibilities. Different can also be the promise of something new—new experiences, new challenges, and new joys.

You may be ready to change… you may have even started making some changes in your life.

But something is still missing. You continue to search for that missing piece, feeling an emptiness, a certain numbness inside, because deep down, you sense there's more — something more to you and your life.

Are You Living Your Best Life?

Imagine waking up each day with joy, creativity, fulfilment, and an innate sense of self. Not just occasionally but every single day. How would it feel to live not just any life, but your truly amazing, beautiful and best life? One that you love, and gives you joy every day.

For you to live a truly beautiful, amazing, fulfilling, uplifting, awesome, best life is a process of discovering yourself and aligning your life with your true authentic self. It's consistently defining and redefining what happiness and fulfilment mean to you. It's about living with intention and making choices that reflect your true self. It's about ensuring that what you do, is meaningful to you.

You may have heard of the phrase 'Your Best Life'. It's a ready-known phrase that's become ubiquitous in self-help literature and motivational speeches, yet its essence cannot be distilled into a one-size-fits-all definition. When I talk about a 'your best life' definition, I like to add adjectives to it to help to define it and give you a sense of what you are aiming for.

Your version of 'truly beautiful, amazing, fulfilling, uplifting, awesome best life' will look very different from mine, and that's exactly how it should be. Your version will be crafted from your own unique self, your spark, your aspirations, values, and experiences. Mine is shaped by my own experiences, my view of the world, what I believe is possible and mixed in different proportions to yours.

Despite these differences, and what we each aim for, I truly believe that living your best life isn't about reaching a destination, it's about the journey itself. It's about committing to a life for yourself that is lived with purpose, passion, and joy.

Or sparkle.

It's where things happen easily for you. And you are navigated by the deep, inner compass of your own values and aspirations. It is a life that aligns perfectly with who you are and everything you aspire to be.

MY JOURNEY TO LIVING MY BEST LIFE

I've always considered myself a happy person, and I thought I was living a truly magnificent, beautiful, amazing, fulfilling, and uplifting life. Yes, I've emerged from a childhood sprinkled with its share of trials. I even spent hours in the high school library pondering future careers. Psychology wasn't just a field that I 'fell into'; it was a deliberate choice reflecting my early curiosity about human behaviour.

Change was never something I feared; in fact, I navigated through eight different careers, and often led transformative initiatives in each. I was a person where I had always felt in command of my life's path, perhaps a 'sparkle' at points. 'At points' is the defining term here. Yet, despite these shifts, I found that I too was living a life on an autopilot of sorts.

Are You Living Your Life on Autopilot?

Uh oh. Yes, I had gathered some of society's achievements, and yes, I was contrary to society in the ways that I had lived. But without realising it, I too was on my own societal conveyor belt, and I had also fallen into some sort of autopilot.

The sense of complete fulfilment for me always seemed transient, fleeting. Sometimes it lingered for a couple of years, other times only a few months. As I evolved, not only did I outgrow roles, but I also confronted the unsettling realisation that my identity had become inextricably linked with my work. This was the beginning of my awakening.

This realisation sparked a crucial question: *'If I am not my work, then who am I?'*

After more than two decades immersed in self-development as a researcher, practitioner, and the subject itself, I faced profound insights about my identity beyond professional labels.

- *'Who was I?'*
- *'What was special about me?'*
- *'Was I truly living my best amazing, uplifting, awesome, life, or one that society approved of?'*

These questions particularly came when I went to drop my daughter off to day-care. Unhappy, upset and not wanting to be there.

These questions also came when I attended meetings at work. You know the ones, where the chairperson is just rolling through the agenda, without any real outcomes, day in, day out.

When I asked myself these questions. I drew blanks on the first two. And the last question, as hard as it was to answer, my answer was *'Society'*.

After some deep introspection and significant life shifts, I find myself today genuinely content and joyful, not just occasionally, but consistently—day in, day out, month after month. It's been this way for several years now, as I have rediscovered myself, and lived a life that I have specifically chosen.

My hope for you is to experience this same sense of deep-seated contentment. To define and live your best life, marked by joy, creativity, mastery, purpose, intent, and happiness—just as I have found.

LET'S BRAIN HACK: ARE YOU LIVING ON AUTOPILOT?

This is a wake-up call for you to take a more conscious role in understanding you, at your deepest level of self, and to ensure that you direct your life.

The way to understand where you are at, is to create awareness for yourself and ask yourself some questions.

One of my favourite ways to do this is through quizzes. Quizzes are a fun gamified way to create awareness of where you are at, so you can start making changes.

Jump online to the **Are you on Autopilot?** quiz using the QR code below or weblink. Once complete, you will receive your own personalised diagnostic report and personalised next steps for you to take.

https://www.bit.ly/autopilotqz

Well done for taking the time to complete this 'hack'.

Use this quiz as a baseline for your progress as you work through this book. Revisit and retake this brain hack periodically to monitor your growth and ensure you are consistently moving towards living a life filled with joy, creativity, and purpose.

Key Highlights of understanding if you're on autopilot

It is so easy to slip into repetitive routines and behaviours, leading to a life on autopilot. By being aware of how we naturally behave, you can recognise the autopilot patterns in your life.

Change brings different. And different is ok. Different can also be awesome. Different can bring possibilities.

You can live with passion and purpose, and you can have a truly beautiful, amazing, fulfilling, uplifting, awesome, best life.

CHAPTER 3

Using Regret as Your Rocket Fuel

When looking back and thinking about their lives, 76% of people regret not taking the actions that would have helped them to discover their true selves. I've read this number many times over. It is such a significant number of people that it makes me sad. It is only one in four people who have lived their lives authentically. Knowing who they truly are and living in alignment with that.

How have we got to a stage in society where this is acceptable? Why are we living today, to a point where we don't know ourselves, or even take a chance to know who we truly are? And why do we just carry on? This is not even something that we talk about.

Ultimate Brain Hacks

Let's look at some of my clients:

Patrick had been working as an accountant for 15 years. He chose this career because it was stable. However, Patrick hates accounting and regrets that he chose it. Now, in his 40s, Patrick feels unfulfilled and stuck in a career that doesn't excite him.

Sarah pursued a career in law because her parents were lawyers. She excelled academically but has never felt passionate about her work. Sarah has a love for environmental conservation, but she stayed in law because of societal and familial expectations. In her mid-30s, Sarah feels disconnected from her career and struggles with a lack of purpose. She envies those who work in fields they are passionate about and wishes she had the courage to follow her own path.

Rachel always dreamed of travelling the world and experiencing different cultures. However, she prioritised her work and responsibilities at home, never finding the right time to travel. As years have passed, Rachel has found herself longing for the adventures she never had, feeling numb and confined by her routine.

Does any of this feel familiar to you?

Nearly everyone I meet has a regret, be it following a career, not changing careers, travelling, being true and authentic with family, not starting a potential passion, staying in a relationship, leaving a relationship, moving, and more.

I want you to stop for a moment and consider who do you want to be? A person who takes the steps to realise their true selves and live in authenticity with that. Or a person like the many of us, who will regret not having done so and many years later, might wake up to how they have been living their life.

What is Regret?

Let's take a step back and look at the importance of the emotion of regret and how we can use regret to make changes to our lives. At its core, regret is an emotion that involves comparing what is, or was, with what could have been. Experiencing regret or having a feeling of regret is a signal that we have deviated from our truest expression of ourselves, our values, or our goals.

Regret, while often uncomfortable, is one of the keys to living a super amazing and awesome life. Regret helps us to reflect on our past choices and our missteps. Regret helps to inform us of our future decisions. It can be used as a catalyst for change, pushing us to pursue opportunities that we might have missed in the busyness of our lives or to make changes to our lives, when we've realised that something does not sit well with us.

Rather than being an emotion that many of us try to avoid, regret can act as a mirror to us, if we allow it to. Regret can reflect our deepest values and unfulfilled desires and guide us towards making more aligned and fulfilling choices now and in the future. It's through the lens of regret that we can see the gaps between where we are now and what could be.

In the narrative of our lives, regret can be a profound teacher if we allow it to be. It asks us to confront our fears. It asks us to acknowledge ourselves. By embracing regret, we can use it to transform it from a source of pain to a powerful motivator for change.

So, let's go back to the opening statistic. 76% of people are not living their life as their true self, but potentially as they believe they are 'supposed' to live.

This doesn't have to be you. Let's take this point as a turning point for you. Let's use any past regrets that you may have, as the rocket-fuel towards a life that is not just lived, but truly lived.

Regret is not the end of your story. Look at it as a beginning. A beginning where you can control your life, make decisions that align with your true self, and create your own future.

Embracing Foresight

One of the most powerful tools is that of 'prospective regret' or foresight. Prospective regret is anticipating what you might regret in the future. It is where you look ahead to your future, and you consider what your future self will feel based on your decisions and actions today.

This is an incredibly powerful brain hack. When you imagine how your future self will look back to now, you build a distance with yourself, allowing you to look at your life and the decisions you face with a different type of clarity that you would not otherwise have. And in the process of doing so, you will more likely make decisions that truly matter, based on the longer term rather than the short-term comfort, that many of us a programmed to fall into.

Using Regret as Your Rocket Fuel

Using foresight is not about living in fear of making mistakes. This is about intentional living. When you recognise that our time is limited and precious, foresight and prospective regret enables you to make the choices that honour our true selves and what we truly desire in life.

MY JOURNEY

Throughout my life, I have found it difficult to regret my past decisions. Sure, sometimes I've stayed in a role too long from a career perspective, but I have always made decisions based on the knowledge I had at the time. Sometimes I may wish I had made a different choice, but one of my mottos is that *'hindsight is never your friend'*. Because of this motto, I often use my mistakes or regrets as learning opportunities.

I find that the feeling of regret will often come up for me in my business. Yes, I've lost clients before they've started working with me, and I've missed opportunities to bring on clients and businesses to work with me, when I should have. It is in those moments where I've felt regret. To work through those feelings; I remind myself that I could only make the decisions and presentations of myself based on my experience, knowledge, and foresight at that moment. When I've experienced this, I've used regret to upskill myself where required, so that the next amazing dream client will say 'yes' to what I offer.

The true secret to what I've been able to achieve through my life and the tool that I use daily is prospective regret. When faced with the decision to leave a job or career, I picture myself five years from that decision and think, *'What would future Simone do?'* It is also a regular sentence I say to myself around the house, particularly when it comes to dishes. Future Simone is always thankful for past Simone for doing the dishes and has never ever had any regrets about doing the dishes, such is the powerful motivator of future Simone.

On a bigger life scale, when buying my first house, I chose a property that we could renovate, subdivide, and live in. This decision was made using prospective foresight. At the time, my partner and I had agreed and were ready to sign the contract for another, more expensive small unit, which was nicer but offered no value-add benefits. By using prospective regret, we made the decision we did. And boy, what a decision it was—it kicked us off on a new life pathway in property investment.

LET'S BRAIN HACK: REGRET

Take a quiet moment and think about your life. Reflect on the different stages and chapters of your journey. As you do, ask yourself:

Do I look back on each stage with happiness, or is there a tinge of sadness?

- Lean into that sadness—why is it there?
- Is there any regret in those moments?
- Where is the regret coming from?

Write down those moments of regret. What were they? Why do you regret those moments?

_____

_____

_____

_____

_____

_____

Pause for a moment. Well done, for moving through this emotion. Acknowledge your courage in facing these feelings.

Now, look at your answers. What actions are you going to take to move forward from those moments where you felt regret? Write them down here:

_____

_____

_____

_____

From this one activity, what new insights have you created for yourself? What new motivations do you now have?

_____

_____

_____

_____

How might you now use this insight to make better decisions in the future?

_____

_____

_____

_____

_____

_____

Well done.

Accept that regret is a part of life, and that it can be a powerful teacher. Forgive yourself for past mishaps and mistakes. Understand that every decision, even those leading to the feeling of regret, was made with the knowledge and circumstances you had at the time.

Key Highlights for using regret as rocket fuel

Regret is a powerful emotion that signals a deviation from our true self. It enables us to reflect on our past choices and helps us to understand our missteps.

Regret can be used as a powerful motivator for change. We can pursue missed opportunities, make amends where necessary, and create new opportunities.

Prospective regret or foresight can be used to anticipate our future regrets right now and enables us to make decisions that align with our truest self.

CHAPTER 4

Brain Basics and How You Create Your World

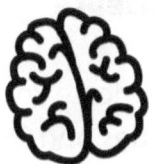

The Brain: Our Own Universe

For everything that we know, the brain is known as the universe's most intricate structure. How? 86 billion neurons are your answer. Let's pause for a moment and take stock. The universe's most intricate known structure consists of 86 billion neurons. Held between our two ears. Every person has their very own universe right between their ears.

And it is our brain that creates our world, how we live, how we see the world, and our environment.

To better understand how the brain works, imagine each neuron (yes, all 86 billion of them) as a switchboard operator in a massive, interconnected city. These operators aren't just passively sitting by; they're actively receiving and processing and sending messages. Not only that, but they can also connect with thousands of other operators, creating a complex network of communication lines. Just as a single message can travel through multiple pathways to reach its destination in a city, each neuron can link up with countless others (imagine thousands of connections per neuron), transmitting signals. It is these transmissions that shape our thoughts, memories, emotions, decisions and action.

Two Pillars within Brain Science

Being the universe's most intricate known structure, it is very easy to get lost in the complexities and intricacies of the brain, from neuronal circuitry to receptor mechanics to genetic and protein expressions, and more.

To understand the concept of brain hacks, living your life on autopilot, and ensuring you become one of the 'awakened' to live the most spectacular and amazing life, we will anchor our understanding of the brain in two foundational concepts: neuroplasticity and the subconscious mind.

It is these two concepts that gives you the key to unlocking your own personal transformation.

A Cheat's Version of Neuroplasticity

Neuroplasticity at its simplest is the process that rewires our brain and in turn, our lives. It was only 25 years ago that scientists thought our brains stopped developing in our early twenties. We now know that the brain is a dynamic, and ever-changing system that adapts through new thoughts, emotions, and experiences.

Neuroplasticity is the process of connecting, disconnecting, and reconnecting of neurons. It's the strengthening and pruning of electrochemical pathways in response to what we think, feel, experience, and learn. This continuous and never-ending process is what allows us to learn new skills, adapt to changes, and overcome challenges throughout our lives.

It is because of neuroplasticity that we have growth, learning, and transformation. This means that the traumas we've had, the stubborn habits that we can't seem to shake, and the fears that hold us back can change. Every new experience, every insight gained, every challenge we face can literally rewire our brains.

Neuroplasticity enables us to deliberately choose to redirect our thoughts and actions. This could be as simple as identifying and adopting a new routine, or challenging yourself with a new experience, or situation, or working through complex problems. Each conscious change strengthens new neural pathways and weakens old ones that no longer serve you. When you learn something – you cannot unknow it again.

So, embrace yourself with the knowledge of neuroplasticity – and know that you can change, from your brain to the outside world.

A Cheats Version to the Subconscious Mind

As much as we like to believe that we fully control our thoughts, our decisions, and lives, we don't.

Consider this: we have around 6,000 thoughts per day. Surprisingly, 95% of these thoughts are driven by our subconscious mind. This means most of our actions, decisions, and reactions—from our daily habits and routines to our spontaneous actions—are happening below the surface, driven by our subconscious mind.

How is that even possible?

Let's break this down. Think about your habits: the way you brush your teeth, your food preferences, how you make and eat your food, the clothes you choose to wear, the routes you take in your daily living; this is all done subconsiously.

Breaking it down further, when you first learned to drive, it required your full attention. All actions were done consciously, from using the accelerator and brakes, to signalling to turn. But now, you can drive to a familiar place without consciously thinking about every turn. Half the time, you may end up at your destination, without remembering the actual drive. Your subconscious mind takes over, guiding you seamlessly.

Let's dive deeper. While you're reading these words on the page, your conscious mind is processing approximately 40-50 pieces of information. That might include the words on these pages, your thoughts about what you're reading, and perhaps a few aspects of your surroundings. Impressive, right?

Brain Basics and How You Create Your World

However, beneath this conscious activity, your subconscious is processing about 11 million bits of information at this very moment. Boom!

So, what exactly is your subconscious up to that you're not aware of?

For starters, it's regulating your breathing, maintaining your heart rhythm, managing your body temperature, controlling your digestion, and keeping tabs on your environment. It consolidates your memories, even while you sleep. Great, but guess what? The subconscious mind doesn't stop there. The subconscious mind also stores our deepest beliefs, habits, and learned behaviours.

It is through the filter of our deepest beliefs, experiences, habits and behaviours that the subconscious processes the immense amount of information our senses absorb every second, allowing only what's most relevant into our conscious mind. This filtering process influences our daily decision-making and emotional responses, often in ways we're not aware of.

Take a moment out now, and answer the following questions:

- Have you ever over-reacted in a meeting for no apparent reason?
- Have you ever had an irrational response to someone doing something that you didn't like?
- Do you experience excessive nerves or panic at the thought of speaking in front of a group, even when the stakes are relatively low?
- Do small losses like misplacing an item, upset you more than they should?

- Have you ever instantly disliked or liked someone without a clear reason?
- Do you find yourself procrastinating on important tasks, feeling almost stuck?

These are all examples of your subconscious mind at work, influencing your behaviour and bypassing your conscious mind.

When we start to understand what's in our subconscious and the filters that our subconscious uses to process the information around us, we can begin to make changes in ourselves. Understanding and working with our subconscious is, I believe, one of the most powerful strategies for creating lasting change.

The Brain: A Master of Energy Efficiency

Despite only making up about 2% of our body's weight, the brain consumes an incredible 20% of our body's energy. This fact alone highlights the immense energy required to manage our thoughts, emotions, behaviours, and bodily functions.

Given the high energy demand of our brains, our bodies face the challenge—how can the brain sustain such intensive activity? The answer to this is through 'shortcuts.' And the brain is the master of creating shortcuts to conserve energy.

These shortcuts enable us to process information and make decisions quickly, without having to engage in energy-intensive thought processes for every decision that we make. The way that we think and perceive everything in our life is based on these shortcuts, 188 different types of shortcuts to be exact.

Brain Basics and How You Create Your World

But what exactly do these shortcuts look like?

Imagine your brain's pathways as the grooves on a record. Each tiny groove represents a pattern of thought or behaviour, and each groove gets played over and over. Just as a record player's needle easily slips into well-worn grooves, our brains default to these established shortcuts, allowing us to operate on autopilot for many of our daily tasks and decisions – this is how 95% of our daily tasks and decisions are made using our subconscious.

Let's Re-Write the Record

The realisation that our brains operate on these energy-saving shortcuts opens a world of possibility for you. Understanding that many of our automatic thoughts and behaviours are simply tracks laid down by repeated use, we can begin the work to consciously create new grooves or to pick the needle up and change a record.

Just as a record can be re-cut with new tracks, our brains can form new connections and pathways, allowing us to change habits, overcome limiting beliefs, and create new insights and ways to filter the information coming in. Let's now do a brain hack to provide new insights, and move the record player's needle to a new track or even change your record.

MY JOURNEY

Consider this scenario: my family and I have just arrived at my in-laws for one of our first family barbecues post-COVID—a significant event, especially for my young daughter who had been anxious about being outside our home. When we arrived, it took some time to get her comfortable, starting with just the two of us playing in the front yard before she was comfortable to join everyone else in the back yard.

Within minutes, she was with her grandfather, and suddenly her face crumpled as she tried to wriggle free from his grip. She then begins to scream. I quickly took her inside to calm her down, while my partner emphatically urged, 'Go, just go—take her and leave.' In less than five minutes, I was packed and in the car, both my daughter and I were upset and hungry.

I was frustrated because I had spent so much time settling her out the front of the house. I had concluded that she just wasn't ready for such a gathering. I felt rushed out of the family event without having any say, hungry and upset, having to deal with a distraught child on my own while my partner stayed behind.

You can imagine the reception my partner received when he returned home later that afternoon.

Let's break what was happening down with some questions that I should've asked myself.

- What did I specifically see happening?
- Were there other things in the scene that I missed because of my past filtering?
- Was I thinking clearly?
- What past experiences could have clouded my judgment?
- What other perspectives hadn't I considered?

There were many layers to the situation, involving several dynamics, that I had dismissed from my consciousness. For instance, my daughter had found a piece of chocolate and was immediately asked to share it with a child she'd never met before — a variable important to her. And one that I didn't consider and immediately dismissed in my story of events.

My partner had witnessed similar scenarios during his own childhood and, recognising the echoes in our daughter's distress, reacted out of a deep sensitivity to both his experiences and our daughter's current discomfort. He had seen the chocolate scenario play out, but in the rush to move my daughter out of the distressing situation, didn't think to explain it to me. Another version that I didn't consider in my story of events.

This single moment, like many we have daily, was packed with complex emotions and tangled interactions that required careful unpacking and understanding from multiple angles.

LET'S BRAIN HACK: IDENTIFYING OUR BRAIN'S SHORTCUTS

This brain hack pulls apart how our brain's shortcuts influence our decisions. By examining a recent decision you've made, you can become aware of your subconscious filters. Using neuroplasticity, you can create new insights and routines to lessen the impact of these shortcuts.

Step 1: Choose a Recent Decision
Think about a recent decision you've made. It could be anything from choosing to try a new product; deciding on a movie to watch; making a career-related choice; or holiday destination.

Write down the decision here:

_____

_____

_____

_____

_____

_____

Step 2: Deconstruct Your Decision

Why did you make the decision that you did?

_____

_____

_____

_____

_____

_____

What steps did you take to get to this decision? Did you do research? Consult with friends? Make a pros and cons list? Or was it simply 'automatic'?

Write your steps to the decision below:

1. _____

2. _____

3. _____

(Add more if necessary)

Step 3: Gather the 'Data' Behind Your Decision

What was the information that contributed to your decision? i.e. - What influenced your decision?

_____

_____

_____

What sources of information did you rely on? Were these sources diverse and reliable?

_____

_____

_____

Was your understanding of the situation complete? Could there have been biases in how you perceived the information?

_____

_____

_____

_____

Did emotions play a role in your decision? If so, how might they have impacted your decision?

_____

_____

_____

_____

Step 4: Explore Alternative Perspectives

Looking at your answers above, what other ways you could have approached this decision?

_____

_____

_____

What other data or who's other perspectives might have been valuable?

_____

_____

_____

How could you have expanded your viewpoint?

_____

Step 5: Re-evaluation
What have you learnt so far? Are there changes you would make to your process? How can you ensure a more balanced and thorough decision-making approach for future?

_____

_____

_____

Well done. By completing this brain hack, you've taken a critical step towards understanding your own brain's shortcuts.

Keep this brain hack in mind as you face future decisions and scenarios that will test you. Remember that taking a step back to analyse your thought process can lead to greater clarity in your decisions.

Key highlights of knowing your brain

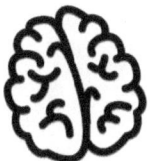

Your brain with its 86 billion neurons, is the universe's most intricate known structure. It's constantly changing and evolving, driving every thought, memory, emotion, and behaviour.

Two key concepts to know about the brain: Neuroplasticity and the Subconscious Mind. Neuroplasticity is the brain's ability to rewire itself through new experiences, thoughts, and challenges. This concept empowers us to change our habits, overcome past traumas, and continuously evolve. 95% of our daily thoughts, decisions, and actions are driven by our subconscious mind. Our subconscious influences our habits, routines, and automatic behaviours, often without our conscious awareness.

Despite its small size, the brain consumes 20% of the body's energy. To manage this, it uses shortcuts or mental pathways that allow for quick decision-making and efficiency, though these can sometimes lead to outdated or unhelpful behaviours.

CHAPTER 5

The Child at the Wheel: Navigating Adult Life with Childhood Maps

Imagine for a moment you're in the driver's seat of a car, navigating the complexities of highways—changing lanes, taking off-ramps, and slowing for traffic. With concentration, and without distraction, for an experienced driver it's quite a complex set of activities that we carry out daily to ensure that we arrive at our destination, safe.

Now, picture that the person steering the car is your seven-year-old self, small hands clutching the wheel, straining to see over the dashboard, trying to make the same complex decisions like changing lanes, taking off-ramps, and overtaking traffic. Just imagining that is enough to know that I don't want to see a seven-year-old version of myself driving a car. With the cognitive development at seven-years-old, I don't know if I would have the capability to navigate the safety aspects of any type of driving activity, other than going straight (if I'm lucky, and I'm not distracted by the cows on the side of the road, or the dog being walked with its owner).

It's extremely dangerous having a seven-year-old at the wheel of the car. Yet metaphorically, this is exactly what we are doing as we work our way through our adult life. The car that you are driving through your life right now, with the highways, off-ramps, and overtaking traffic, is driven by no other than your seven-year-old self.

How We Form Our Maps

From the moment we are born, our brains start to make sense of the world around it. This sense-making is built by our immediate environment. The words we hear, the behaviours we observe, and the emotions expressed around us all contribute to the foundational beliefs we carry into our adulthood. These environmental cues shape our early experiences and form the maps that then guide us through our life.

These maps are our first blueprints for understanding life, influencing how we see ourselves, how we approach obstacles, and how we think and feel. These maps influence not only our internal world, but also how we interact with the external world around us. They shape our career choices, our relationships, our health behaviours, our dreams and what we believe is possible for us.

The Child at the Wheel: Navigating Adult Life with Childhood Maps

A simplistic representation of the maps in action, is of a child frequently praised for their efforts, may form the initial pathways and maps for confidence and security. They may grow into an adult with a growth mindset, seeing challenges as opportunities to learn and expand. In contrast, a child who is often criticised may form neural pathways and maps around self-doubt, and constantly not feeling good enough. They may develop limiting beliefs that persist into adulthood, questioning their capabilities and worth.

Diving in further, if your early experiences taught you to avoid risk and seek safety, you might find yourself staying in a job you don't love, simply because it's secure. Or you might stay in a relationship longer than you should because the fear of the unknown is greater than the discomfort of the present.

Looking at yourself, think about how you react in stressful situations. Is there a pattern playing out there? Think about how you interact with others, or even how you perceive yourself. Are any of these responses based on specific experiences that you can remember in your childhood?

Recognising that the origins of our beliefs and the maps that we use to filter the information of our current environment stem from our childhood enables us to question which of these beliefs serve us and which limit us. By reflecting on our early childhood environments, our experiences and the influential figures of our childhood, we can begin to discern which parts of our belief system are truly ours and which are borrowed from the magical big people of our past.

MY JOURNEY

Despite studying the brain and working on myself for over 20 years, my whole world is still based on the maps that were first constructed in my childhood.

Here are a few tangible examples across a wide range of beliefs and fears that detail how pervasive your childhood experiences can affect you today.

My Daughter and Spiders
We are born with one fear, and only one fear. This one fear is common to all of us. Every other fear is therefore a construct that we have developed through life. Knowing this fact and watching my daughter grow up has been fascinating. As a toddler, she was fascinated with spiders. When she saw a spider, she would reach out to it with curiosity, wanting to touch it. When spiders were around, I showed interest and curiosity alongside her.

By the age of three, she was petrified of spiders. Screaming when one appeared. A stark difference to 12 months prior. Unfortunately, grandma, who would often look after my daughter, has an immense fear of spiders. To where she would exclaim, 'I don't like spiders', and shiver every time, just with the thought of spiders, let alone a toy or a real spider.

I Can't Run
The *'I can't run'* belief has been a narrative that I have used throughout my whole life. When I was in grade one at school

The Child at the Wheel: Navigating Adult Life with Childhood Maps

on a school sports day, we divided ourselves into groups to do a run around the oval. By this early age, I had already worked out that I ran slower than others. Perhaps this was because I tried a few weeks of Jazz Ballet at the age of five, when I hadn't fully developed my coordination at that age, to then be told to come back in a year. Perhaps it was because I was still developing my coordination in running.

I segmented myself into the 'slower' group. Unfortunately, the fast group and the slow group were not the same size. The two parent helpers ushered me into the fast group, because I was tall for my age. The outcome, I made the oval run, about 50 metres behind the pack, hyperventilating, unable to breathe, in tears. A brown paper bag was bought over to me, to breathe through for the next few minutes.

From that moment, PE became my most despised class in school. I was always the last picked for teams, the last in races, the last in everything. In my early adulthood, the narrative developed further to 'I just don't exercise'.

When my fit partner suggested in our mid-20's that he was starting a futsal team, and 'Would I like join?', there was a lot of hesitation on my behalf. Hesitation, because I had never been a part of a team sport before. And hesitation, because *'I don't exercise'* and *'I can't run'*.

When I joined the team, which position did I take? That's right, the goalie. The position with the least amount of running, because 'I don't exercise' and 'I can't run'. After a few years,

I ventured out of the goals, and onto the field, dissolving the *'I don't exercise'*. However, the *'I can't run'* narrative had changed to, *'I must trick my brain in order to run'*.

Simone the Tight-A***
Growing up in a single-parent household, money was always tight. To prepare for Christmas, my mum would always put away $5 every week to be able to afford the Christmas meal. When I was old enough for a job, I got not one, but three jobs to put myself through university, paying for my train travel, and my books, while loading up on the HECS debt. As a PhD student on a stipend in my early 20s, I made it work living out of home through scrimping and saving. A night out was going to the local pub down the road with its $4 pizzas.

This type of lifestyle led me to be stingier than anything. I didn't spend money. The narrative that I had was that *'Money was not to be spent. It was to be saved'*. And so, I saved.

To buy a house, with a mortgage and monthly interest repayments required a significant mindset shift. To start my investing journey in property, required a complete change in mindset.

The Food You Eat
My favourite meal is spaghetti bolognaise. The richness of the meat with the tomato sauce, topped with parmesan cheese. If my son has not eaten his toast in the morning, I cannot go past finishing his last few bits with the vegemite

The Child at the Wheel: Navigating Adult Life with Childhood Maps

and butter… yes, I'm ashamed to say, even if it's a few hours old. It always gets to me.

The food that I eat today is a product of what was fed to me as a child. Spaghetti bolognaise was served on a weekend, as a family. So even though the memories may be long forgotten, the neuronal pathways running the spaghetti bolognaise loop are still there. Same with my vegemite toast as a child. In fact, all your favourite food comes down to your first experience of having that food, and the feelings that you felt, and your experience of it.

The opposite is true. You won't ever see me eating some kids' favourites, the 'teeth lollies', due to an episode of gastro I had soon after having tried one as a six year old.

LET'S BRAIN HACK: IDENTIFYING THE MAPS CREATED BY YOUR SEVEN-YEAR-OLD-SELF

Let's start the process of identifying, challenging, and updating the mental maps created in childhood that no longer serve you now.

Step 1: Identify What You'd Like to Work On
Identify an area of your life that you'd like to work on. It could be anything to do with work, career, love, relationships, your children, finances, wealth, fitness, health, self, self-confidence, happiness, your dreams, goals or something else.

_____

_____

Step 2: Identify Your Beliefs
Write down all your beliefs around that area. List them.

_____

_____

_____

_____

_____

Step 3: Review Your Beliefs
Look at your list of beliefs. What commonalities are there?

_____

_____

_____

_____

_____

Can you identify which beliefs you've borrowed from someone else? If so, who?

_____

_____

_____

_____

_____

Can you identify the experiences that these beliefs came from? List them here.

_____

_____

_____

_____

_____

Which beliefs serve you for the positive? Which beliefs do you no longer want to keep?

_____

_____

_____

_____

_____

Step 4: Challenge Your Belief

Choose one belief or behaviour you've identified as not helpful to you moving forward.

Now, question the belief with yourself: Is this belief true?

_____

Now, question the belief with yourself again - Is it really true?

_____

Question the belief with yourself again - Who is it true for?

_____

Question yourself again – If it's not true, what is true?

_____

Commit to challenging this belief for the next month. This could involve:

- Practicing affirmations that reinforce a new, empowering belief.
- Discussing your findings with a supportive friend to gain new perspectives.
- Journalling.

Write down below, how you will challenge this belief?

_____

_____

_____

_____

Step 5: Review
Pop a reminder in your calendar to review in one month with the page number of this book.

After a month, review and reflect:

How has challenging and updating this belief affected you?

_____

_____

_____

_____

The Child at the Wheel: Navigating Adult Life with Childhood Maps

What new behaviours or thought patterns have you adopted in the past month?

_____

_____

_____

How do you feel about the belief now compared to when you started?

_____

_____

_____

What other beliefs or behaviours are you now inspired to challenge and update? Write them down and repeat this exercise.

_____

_____

_____

_____

Well done. This process is ongoing. Celebrate the progress you've made and consider setting new challenges for yourself, continuing to re-draw your neural maps towards a life that truly reflects who you are today.

Key Highlights for navigating your life with childhood maps

Our childhood experiences form mental maps that guide our decisions and actions throughout life. These early-formed neuronal pathways solidify over time, becoming subconscious scripts that dictate our responses to various situations.

These early maps influence not only our internal world but also our external world, such as career choices, relationships, and health behaviours.

Recognising the origins of our beliefs allows us to discern which ones serve us and which limit us, enabling us to be able to upgrade our maps.

CHAPTER 6

Drop Your Crap

Before we can truly know and align ourselves to who we truly are, we need to clear our clutter—or as I like to call it, the 'crap'. This is the crap that does not add to our lives that fills our minds, lives, and physical spaces. One of my favourite proverbs when it comes to crap is, *'You can't keep filling a cup, if it's already full'*. Meaning that there is nothing more to add to it. If it's full, it's full. A bit like our minds.

Holding onto our own crap can make your mind full and when your mind is full, not much more can be added into it. Now's the time to empty that cup to make room for something better. Because our mind and our lives cannot take on anything new, if we are already full.

By dropping our crap, we naturally reconnect back to ourselves. When we are clear, empty and ready to fill, our eyes are open to the opportunities that we might miss amid our own crap, chaos, and busyness. If you're still not sure of the impact that holding onto crap has on you, then take a moment and answer these questions:

- Have you ever felt anxious or stressed, when you've had too much going on at work, with family, or in your personal life?
- Have you ever felt overwhelmed when your environment is cluttered?
- Have you been exhausted, thinking of and not moving past grudges or regrets?
- How much time do you waste on activities that don't bring you joy or fulfilment?
- Have you ever felt overwhelmed by the constant stream of notifications, alerts and emails?
- Are you tired of juggling so many roles and responsibilities?
- Have you ever suffered from 'paralysis by analysis' leading to indecision from you overthinking?

When people think of crap, they naturally think of physical clutter. And yes, I put my hand up to this. Yes, I am a person who is known to have clutter. In the corporate world, a photo of my desk with all the clutter was showcased to the organisation in LEAN presentations. Ha, ha. Even now, I still live and work with clutter around me. Yes, I still have my own work to do.

When I talk about crap, I am also talking about all the other non-physical crap. This is the mental and emotional crap, the time crap, the digital crap. It fills our spaces, our calendars, our minds, our emotions… and that's about it.

The crap we have is often hiding in plain sight. Most of the time, we choose to not be aware of it and avoid the real reason it is there. It just dissolves into the landscape and haze of what is our lives, and we muddle along, swimming in it.

Having too much, is what keeps us stuck and limits the opportunities we see right in front of us. And the opportunity right now for you, is to live a super amazing life.

Why We Accumulate Crap

When we take a moment to look deeper, there is often a subconscious need or pattern playing out with our crap. There are many 'whys' for why we accumulate crap, with some listed below. As you read them, notice your response to each.

The Security Blanket
For many, our crap can often act as a form of security blanket, where each item represents memories, or relationships or achievements in our lives. The crap object will then serve as the tangible proof of our experience or feelings from that memory.

Often, the thought of letting go of the item or connection can sometimes feel like losing a part of yourself or your past. This is particularly true for items with sentimental value, where discarding them might seem akin to discarding the associated memories and relationships. This can be items that were given to you for your birthday, or Christmas, or by a particular someone, jewellery and photos.

Look around your space at these items. I challenge you to answer, will you lose who you are, and your memory, without that item?

Fear of Not Having Enough

Have you ever found yourself holding onto items, 'just in case'. This can be driven by a fear of 'not having enough' and is particularly prevalent if you've experienced difficult times in the past, such as financial hardship, food insecurity, or emotional deprivation. The crap we can't let go of, is your protection against potential future shortages, a way to feel secure now, and into the future.

Think of the spare bed, bed linen and pillows, when no one has crashed at your house in the last ten years… Or the tent, snow gear, or old work clothes, in case we go camping, go to the snow, work back in that industry again (yes – I am guilty of holding onto that waitressing apron, ten years after having my last hospitality job… and let's not talk about the laboratory coat that I still have).

These items are usually in the back of your closets or spare rooms, or garage. When you look at these items with renewed eyes, I challenge you to ask yourself: do you really need it now? And will you need it in the next 24 months?

Items of Perceived Value

We often perceive the value that our crap is 'worth so much' and therefore we will not let it go. However, what we pay for an item and the value that we perceive it to have years later, are often not the same. We might hold onto an old piece of furniture, a technology gadget, or item of clothing because we remember the price tag when we bought it.

The other narrative that we might play is *'if we were to sell it sometime, it's it's worth this amount'.* Hello wedding party dresses, formal wear, shoes, hair pieces, old phones, cameras, furniture and more.

Once again, these items can be found in the back of drawers, closets, rooms that are not used, and sheds. When you look at these items, ask yourself: *'does it still have a purpose in your life?'*

Wounds of our Past

Just like physical clutter, the scars of our past occupy mental space preventing us from moving forward and living fully in the present. An example of this might be to avoid further occurrence of 'pain', we often hold onto our past hurts, grievances, or trauma without fully processing them. I often call this 'the wounds of our past'. They drag us down. And filter a negative view on our life.

For instance, a decision made in the workplace years ago might continue to affect your current approach to similar situations, causing you to regularly act defensively or with undue caution.

Look at your behaviour in the workplace, in relationships, friendships, and with family. What wounds may you still be carrying around?

Over Committing

How often do you find yourself saying 'yes', even when your calendar, your work, your life may already be overflowing with commitments, whether in terms of time, energy, or responsibilities? This tendency to over commit could result from many reasons; a desire to please others; an inability to say no; or even a fear of missing out.

When we are constantly busy, we might find ourselves unproductive, not achieving what we set out to do, stretched thin by our numerous obligations. We may even find ourselves turning away, and procrastinating. The constant feeling of busyness leaves little room for the activities to move us forward, or the activities that make us happy, or moments of relaxation.

Look at your calendar, are you over committed in any areas of your life?

Types of Crap

To understand where the crap may hide in your life, I've listed some categories to enable you to understand what forms of crap there are, so you can start the process to drop your crap.

Physical Crap

Physical crap is the most visible form that we see (or choose not to see) around us. It's found in our home, outside our home, our office or workspace, our cars (hello discarded food wrappers), our garages, even our childhood memorabilia that may be stored stored in our former homes. This can include the clothes you never wear, old gadgets that have been replaced, unused furniture, the cutlery drawer, the closet, children's clothes, books, papers, containers, medicines, and more.

Digital Crap

This is often a hidden category, because it's unseen and not physically present in our environment. It includes everything from overcrowded email inboxes to sprawling photo collections on social media, the apps that we no longer use and, the 'friends' we keep online. Additional digital crap can be unwanted newsletters, digital files and cookies.

Time Crap

These are the time wasters, the activities that take our time and give nothing in return, leaving us drained and dissatisfied. It includes unnecessary meetings, emails, long commutes that could be calls, or activities that we attend out of obligation rather than enjoyment.

Mental and Emotional Crap
Mental and emotional crap may be the hardest to work through, as it requires deep introspection and potentially difficult decisions. It includes toxic relationships, or guilt-inducing activities that no longer serve us. It also includes the emotional baggage that we can't let go of.

Clearing our crap and deciding what to let go of can be a lengthy process. To shed bucketloads of physical items, digital crap, clearing calendars and more can take several months, or even years.

So, how do you start?

With one item. Whether it's an old stained-jumper, or your social network, or the cutlery drawer. Each item, physical, emotional or time bound, opens your mind, your life, creates clarity and opens the door to the next opportunity.

MY JOURNEY

Over the years, my mindset has always been that you can do anything, to live life as full as possible; dream big and play big, 'to have it all'. And that is certainly how I have lived for the first many years of my life. By looking at me and my life, you would say that I lived a very 'full' life.

Following the birth of my wonderful, beautiful and gorgeous daughter, my internal world had changed. My identity had changed. My sense of self had changed. Despite my new time commitments to my daughter, I tried to continue life as before. This included returning to a demanding work- as many hours that is possible, everything is a priority, but not enough resources full-time job. This job, alongside maintaining previous relationships, community volunteer positions, sports and other obligations did not leave room for the new realities that I faced of motherhood.

It wasn't the busyness or the stress that signalled the need for change, but the repeated and constant presence of illnesses—a clear message from my subconscious that something needed to change.

Inspired by the Marie Kondo craze at the time, I embarked on my year of clearing. It was a transformative process. Eighty-four garbage bags of crap were donated to charity. Additional pieces of furniture, and other assortments were left out on the kerb – we called it 'roadside treats', picked up by passersby for their own use — which now became their crap.

From a time perspective, I created a 'no' board. It kept the concept of saying 'no' very present and front of mind. For every meeting, every item of work that I said no, or delegated to someone else, I wrote the equivalent time saving on the board. In a single month, I had said no to 60 hours of work, and meetings. No wonder I was feeling stretched beyond measure, and sick.

Drop Your Crap

Over the course of the year, I said 'goodbye' to friendships and activities that did not fulfil me, creating space for my daughter, and my new life that was unfolding before my eyes.

One day, seemingly out of nowhere, I felt the urge to get my eyes lasered. It was something I had always said I would do 'someday', and that 'someday' had finally arrived now that I was much lighter. I also found the space to start a business. Learning the ropes of entrepreneurship took energy, mental capacity, and time—resources I now had, thanks to the space I had created in my life.

My most recent clearing the crap from my life has resulted in over 1,000 items leaving my physical space and a thorough declutter of my business. The result of my latest clear out of crap, is this book.

What might the opportunity be for you, once you clear your crap?

LET'S BRAIN HACK: DROP YOUR CRAP

Your mission?

Clear your crap. It may seem too simplistic to be a brain hack. But often the simplest can be the most effective.

Through this process, not only will you reclaim physical and mental space, but you'll also open doors to new possibilities.

Grab your **Clear Your Crap** scorecard here to work through your crap and tally it up! Jump onto the QR code below.

Once you start counting the items – it's easy to get hooked.

https://www.afreshapproach.com.au/clearyourcrap

Key Highlights of Drop Your Crap

Clearing physical, mental, and emotional crap out of your life creates the space for growth and opens you to new opportunities, and a deeper connection with your true self.

If we can understand why we hold on to our own crap; whether it's for security, a perceived value, or emotional attachment helps us to address the true cause for our clutter. This can help us to let go of our crap and move forward.

In clearing our crap, constant vigilance is the key. This is not a one-time event, but a continuous process of identifying and removing what no longer serves you to open you up to opportunities.

CHAPTER 7

Peeling Back the Layers of You

What is the persona that you present to the world? You know what I'm talking about – this is the mask that you wear for others hoping they will appreciate and admire you. Or perhaps you present the 'poor little me' mask in the hope of gaining attention and connection?

- What specific opinion are you seeking to evoke?
- What parts of you are you trying hide from the world?

These questions may be direct and bring about uncomfortable emotions in you right now. Or perhaps you are thinking – *'that's not me'*. Or perhaps you are glossing over these questions, because right now, they make little sense to you.

Ultimate Brain Hacks

I have come to realise that everyone projects a persona or mask to the world, which may or may not be true to their inner self. It may be all the time that you project this persona, and you don't even know that you do. Or it may be only in certain situations.

Let's understand the persona that you project, with some further questions:

- What do you project when you are at work?
- Is it different from who you are at home?
- Who are you in social situations?
- Is it different to who you are one on one?
- Or when you are with extended family?

Are you surprised by some of your answers? Intrigued? If you need to, go back and reread the first part of this chapter again, with a pen and paper. Write whatever comes to you as you answer each question.

We are now working to peel the layers of yourself and create an understanding of yourself at the deepest level. This process of self-discovery is a journey that I believe everyone must go through and is vital for several reasons. First, by understanding who we truly are, and the persona that we present to the world; we can make a conscious decision to bring our authentic selves to the world more often. Second, it allows us to understand our motivations. The motivations that we know about… and the motivations hidden from our conscious mind.

This work is the key to unlocking your mind and living a more aligned, richer, deeper, meaningful and happier life. And many times, a longer life. Wearing a mask or upholding a persona can have significant consequences to our health, and how we live our lives. Perhaps it has already impacted you, without you being aware that you are wearing a mask?

The effort to maintain a façade is not only exhausting, but can lead to severe burnout. The strain of presenting as someone or something different to what you truly are (knowingly or unknowingly) can often accompanied by physical symptoms, and down the track other issues that impact your health. Ugh.

Beyond the physical and psychological toll, the mismatch between our persona and our authentic self can lead us to losing our sense of our self. It can cause many of our self-sabotage patterns, and the experience of repeated groundhog loops throughout our life.

If we were to shed our masks and present our true selves, the imperfect, raw versions of ourselves to the world - we foster deeper, more fulfilling relationships, enrich our experiences and open new opportunities that we cannot even begin to imagine right now.

Let's peel back our layers and find our true, authentic selves. Are you ready to open this Pandora's box of sorts?

Peeling the Layers of Our Self

The onion is often used as a metaphor for the layers of the self. However, there's an aspect of this metaphor that is often overlooked; as we peel away the layers, it might sometimes hurt. Your eyes may sting a little. And that's okay. You have permission to hurt. You have permission to cry.

Peeling back the layers of our identity is a process that could completely shift every aspect of everything that we thought that we knew about ourselves. It requires us to confront and understand the various parts of us and why they present the way they do. So, like an onion, let's begin with the outermost layer, our persona, and work to peel that back.

1. The Persona

The persona is the face that we present to the world. It is how we knowingly or unknowingly want others to perceive us. The persona can be so deeply intertwined with our true self, that for many of us, we don't realise that we have a persona, and that there is more to us than what we present the world.

We often start showing our persona in early childhood. Think about the times when you've been told to do something, not because you want to, but because it's expected of you. Like: 'Go, say hello to Aunty Helen', or told to 'say sorry', when we're not even sure what we're saying sorry for. Or as a child, we're told to 'put on a happy face', or 'just smile', when we're angry or frustrated.

This persona carries into our adulthood. Think about wearing a certain attire to work, or in a meeting at work, suppressing your honest opinion because of expectations. What about projecting that your life is all happiness and joy on social media? We also create a persona to fit our roles that we have in life. This could be mother, father, daughter, son, brother, sister, career person.

This persona or mask that we wear is just that. A persona, and not the real you. There is so much more to you, underneath that. It's time to let that shine through.

Peeling Back the Layers of You

2. The Shadow Self
The words, 'shadow self' sends a few chills, doesn't it?

Beneath the surface, beneath the mask, we encounter our shadow self. The parts of us that we choose to hide from others, and not show the world. Most of the time, we will deny that it even exists.

This shadow self holds all the things that we don't like about ourselves. It holds our deepest and darkest fears, never uttered to anyone or even ourselves, unexpressed anger, or even talents and deep desires we've suppressed in our need for acceptance. It can hold our most inner vulnerabilities, and the scars left by past traumas and unmet needs.

Much of our shadow self lies in the subconscious, because we barely want to know about it. But this is where the real magic lies. Looking at what sits in our shadow self can brings us understanding, clarity and choice. By acknowledging and nurturing our shadow, we can heal and release patterns that no longer serve us.

3. The Authentic Self
Beneath all the layers, societal expectations, the masks, our fears, our shadows, is our true authentic self, the purest expression of who we are. It's where our innate desires, passions, talents and abilities reside, untainted by the external world.

Discovering and aligning with your authentic self is the ultimate act for yourself. It is where the true magic lies, and it is the way for a life lived with purpose, integrity, amazingness, laughter, and fulfilment.

The journey towards discovering and connecting with your authentic self isn't merely about unmasking and discarding the roles you've been taught to play, but about deeply reconnecting with your inner essence and rediscovering the dreams you may have put aside in order to fit in.

Embracing your authentic self allows you to tap into your true energy, vitality, flow, and creativity. When you live a life of authenticity, your decisions become more intuitive and aligned. Living in alignment with your authentic self, will attract relationships that are rich in sincerity and understanding, as we naturally gravitate towards others who resonate with our truest selves and we start to create our own magic.

Who wouldn't want to live that life?

The Creation of the Shadow Self, and Our Persona

- How is it that we get to a point where we hide parts of ourselves from ourselves and the world?
- Why do we present a persona to the world that is anything less than our most authentic self?
- And how do we reach a point, where we do not even recognise, or know how to access our most authentic self?

Gabor Maté's work provides some insights into why this happens. In our early formative years, the need for both connection and authenticity are fundamental to us. Yet, these two core needs can be at odds with each other, with often our need for connection overpowering our need for authenticity.

From birth our early relationship connections, primarily with our caregivers, lay the groundwork for our sense of security, self-worth, and our capacity for authentic relationships later in life.

Peeling Back the Layers of You

Neurologically, these relationship connections stimulate the release of neurotransmitters like oxytocin, known as the love hormone, which fosters bonding and reduces stress. The quality of these early interactions and connections with others influences the development of neural pathways that govern our emotional regulation, stress responses, and even our susceptibility to addiction.

The suppression of our authenticity is a complex, multi-faceted process that occurs without our conscious awareness and begins early on through very subtle experiences. For example, as children, we learn to adjust behaviour based on the approval or disapproval of our caregivers. For example, if the authentic expression of ourselves is met with negative reactions, we start to suppress aspects of our ourselves. Even simple comments like 'stop crying' or 'don't be silly' starts the process to develop our personas and move us away from our authenticity.

Adding further complexity, we also mimic the behaviours, attitudes, and responses of those around us, further suppressing our authenticity. This pattern expands to include societal expectations as we grow, pressing us to fit into societal norms and unspoken expectations.

As adults, recognising and unravelling these complex layers is not a linear process; it's cyclical and ongoing. Each layer that we explore brings us closer to our authentic self, but also reveals new layers to uncover. As we work through each layer, we are upgrading our maps, with an adult lens.

MY JOURNEY TO THE CORE

The path to my core started many years ago, through the many career changes that I had, each time believing that I was following my own path. And yes, there have been moments of deep introspection where I've confronted the realities that I had constructed around myself. Many of those moments were catalysed from a single comment or insight that tore apart everything I had known until that point. Cue, a good friend saying to me in my early 20s, 'I hardly know anything about you'. Or the realisation of how circular narratives in my head were playing out in my behaviour at work, and how people perceived and interacted with me.

Even with these many realisations and continuing to peel back the layers of my masks, little had I known that as I was travelling through life, I had crafted a persona. A mask that I was not aware of its existence until it was pointed out by a mentor, and this mask was at complete odds with my real, genuine self. That single observation ignited an intense self-exploration aimed at uncovering my true self. Because if I wasn't me, or the construct of who I thought was me, who was I? And If I wasn't that, what was hiding underneath all of that?

During this time, I pondered the moments when I felt genuinely happy and at peace around others. I questioned the authenticity of my expression in all types of activities, wondering what made them feel so real, or not. I noticed patterns in my behaviour, times when I was more performer than participant, acting in ways I believed were expected of me rather than being driven my 'real' self. I examined past interactions where I realised that I had a facade. I worked out that I felt onstage whenever I felt a slight unease within myself. This could be in social gatherings, at parties, at work, or in various instances with family.

I talked to my identified authentic connections, asking them what they saw of me, and what they saw of this performance. The deeper I delved into discussions about this 'mask' concept, the clearer it became that much of my life had been a performance, shaped by my experiences and societal expectations.

This persona that I had created and lived as for so long was characterised by traditionally masculine traits like achievement, analytical thinking, logic, determination, keeping to oneself, and not expressing feelings. This persona was created in my childhood, being in an all-female household, with very feminine energy surrounding me. To balance that, I naturally, began the path towards more masculine traits, studying mathematics, science, and looking down on any crying that anyone might exhibit for any reason. The shadow self, subconsciously telling me *'that if I was good enough, and achieved enough, then perhaps the father who had left the household, would love me'.*

This self-reflection helped me uncover the hidden layers of my authentic self, that my persona had hidden for so long. I discovered at my core inherent qualities such as empathy, sensitivity, intuition, and nurturing—traits I had unintentionally suppressed until that point. Unveiling these aspects of myself has been transformative.

Rather than completely discarding my old mask, I have learned to integrate all parts of my self. Today, I am still discovering aspects of myself, why I behave certain ways in situations, why I get angry in others, and what needs I might be trying to get subconsciously in those instances.

Today, the Simone you see differs vastly from the person I was before this journey began. I no longer present myself as a one-dimensional character but embrace my multifaceted nature. This change hasn't been about becoming someone else; it is a return to my true self—a homecoming to the person I truly am.

LET'S BRAIN HACK: EMBRACING YOUR AUTHENTICITY

We are peeling back each layer to uncover the real you. The you that sits behind the persona or mask that you present to the world. Be gentle with yourself in this process. It can take time.

Finding Your Persona
Sit in a quiet spot and try answering these questions. The answers may not come to you immediately but allow yourself to ponder on them.

What are the situations in which you most frequently wear a mask?
- Think about the times when you felt awkward or uncomfortable? Perhaps at work? Or in specific situations at work? Meetings? Or perhaps playing sports? Or perhaps with various family members?
- What did you do in those situations? Put the 'armour on'? Talk logically and analytically? Laugh, because you thought you had to?

_____

_____

_____

_____

Revealing Your Shadow Self

What parts of yourself are you hesitant to acknowledge or show to others?

These could be traits, desires, or past experiences. Write them down, no matter how uncomfortable it might feel.

_____

_____

_____

_____

_____

_____

If you struggle with answering this, then ask yourself the following questions:

What feelings/situations/scenarios do I avoid?

_____

_____

Peeling Back the Layers of You

_____

_____

What truths am I not facing about myself?

_____

_____

_____

What deep lying fears might I have that prompt me to put the façade in what I've written about above?

_____

_____

_____

What am I hiding? And why do I feel that I need to hide it?

_____

_____

_____

Finding Your Authentic Self

Consider what values, passions, and aspirations are most important to you, regardless of external influences.

- What makes you uniquely you?
- Who are you really?

Write about these core aspects of your authentic self.

_____

_____

_____

_____

_____

_____

If you have trouble answering these questions, consider asking the people closest to you. Ask them in what situations do they see you presenting a mask to the world? What is that mask? And what is it, that makes you uniquely you?

Integration and Acceptance

How you can integrate and accept all aspects of yourself. What steps can you take to embrace your whole self in daily life?

Identify one small action you can take this week to live more authentically. This could be as simple as expressing a hidden talent or sharing a part of yourself you usually keep private.

Write down your action here.

_____

_____

_____

Celebrate
At the end of the week, look at your experience. Did you do it? How did it feel to take that step towards authenticity?

_____

_____

_____

What did you learn about yourself? How can you continue to live out your truth in other areas of your life?

_____

_____

_____

This is a very small snapshot of being able to identify the three layers of yourself.

Understanding yourself is a lifelong journey.

This is about embracing the full person that you are, the shadow, and the authentic you, and aligning your persona or mask with the true authentic you, and shadow self. It doesn't end with finding the core but continues as you choose to live out your truth in every aspect of your life.

For me, I have found this journey challenging and rewarding, and I hope that you do too.

Key highlights to journey to your core

We are multi-faceted and multi-layered. The outermost layer - the persona is the face we present to the world, often masking our true feelings and vulnerabilities. Recognising this is a mask helps us understand that we can uncover our true selves beneath the surface.

The shadow self are the parts of us that we hide from the world, including our deepest fears, hidden beliefs, unexpressed anger, shadow values, and suppressed desires. By acknowledging and nurturing our shadow self, we can heal and release patterns that no longer serve us, leading to greater self awareness and authenticity.

At the core of our being lies our authentic self, the purest expression of who we are, free from external influences and societal expectations. Embracing our authentic self allows us to live a life filled with purpose, integrity, and fulfilment, fostering deeper connections and inspiring others to do the same.

CHAPTER 8

Meet the Real You

- Have you ever met the real you?
- Do you know who the real you is?
- What are your deepest passions and interests?

To truly know yourself, you need to peel back the layers of societal expectations, past conditioning, and external pressures and get to the heart of you. Past your persona, past your shadow and to your core. The heart of living in true alignment is a congruence between your inner self and the life you lead. It's where your actions, decisions, and life direction are in harmony with your authentic self—reflecting your values, passions, and purpose.

True alignment with your self transcends societal expectations and the confines of what you believe you should do. It is where you make choices that mirror your deepest desires and true calling. It is where your subconscious and conscious selves speak to each other. This is where the magic happens—where happiness and fulfilment are not just pursued but truly lived.

The transformation that comes with alignment of your conscious and subconscious selves extend far beyond a single activity. Living in alignment allows you to move through life with purpose and intention, creating ripples of positive change around you. You inspire those around you. You are a living example of what is possible when one lives true to their essence.

Expressing the Real You

- How do you know that you are expressing the realest authentic you?
- How do you know if you're working in alignment with your subconscious?
- How can you tell if you're on your natural and aligned life path?

When you're living as your most authentic self, you'll feel a profound sense of confidence, an innate understanding and a powerful drive that *'you've got this'*. This feeling is not just a fleeting emotion but a deep-rooted conviction that you are exactly where you need to be, doing exactly what you are meant to do.

When you're in alignment with yourself, your intuition — essentially your subconscious radar lights up. Often referred to as a 'gut feeling', intuition is the subconscious processing signals, giving us a full body *'yes'*, or perhaps a hint of hesitation, or even a full *'no'*. This intuitive guidance helps you navigate life's decisions with clarity and ease, as it reflects your true desires and innermost values.

In Western society, we've been programmed to prioritise our cerebral thinking. Thinking with our brain. Thinking logically. Analytically. Over analysing. So much so, that we've lost touch with our ability to absorb and respond to the world subconsciously, to be led by our bodies, our hearts, our gut, rather than our minds. This has led many of us becoming disconnected from our true selves.

When we do not work in alignment with our true self, we will find that we will self-sabotage, create blocks, feel bouts of unexplained unhappiness or anger, and at times experience physical symptoms.

So, how do we get to know ourselves and ensure that our conscious and subconscious mind are in sync? How can we ensure that we are in alignment with ourselves?

Start with the intent to know yourself. Listen to the whispers that you often dismiss before they are fully formed. Pay attention to your body's whispers (or screams and yells!). The physical whispers, niggles, aches, pains, sores, injuries will often reveal your true feelings and instincts. Notice how you and your body react in different situations—do you feel relaxed and energised, or tense and drained?

When faced with a decision, pause and tune into your inner voice. Ask yourself quietly, *'how does each option make you feel?'* Does it ignite excitement and passion, or does it evoke a sense of dread and resistance? Listen to that, and act on it.

Initially, it may feel scary to listen to these signals. It may be even scarier to act and make decisions based on these signals. Especially if this is the first time you have ever taken heed of what your subconscious is telling you.

As you align you and your life with your subconscious, and you embrace more and more of your authentic self, you will find that your actions become more intentional, your relationships more genuine, and your life more meaningful.

Enjoy this journey of self-discovery, where you learn to trust yourself and your intuition. By prioritising this inner alignment, you create a life that resonates with your true self, filled with purpose, joy, and unwavering confidence.

MY JOURNEY

My path to aligning with my true self has meant reshaping my career and my life. I have had tough decisions to make. One of those was to confront the reality of my professional life.

While my career was marked by external success and recognition, at times, it contrasted with my inner values and deepest desires. The pivotal moment came when I decided to leave the security and prestige of my well-paying, well-recognised job to venture into a domain that truly spoke to my soul.

Following another frustrating meeting, I heard the subconscious whisper: *'What if it doesn't have to be like this?'*

A little bit cheeky. A little bit playful. The impact of listening to my subconscious is not to be understated. Yes, I did freak out. Yes, it took me three weeks to act on this and resign. Yes, I was scared. Scared for what my future held. And scared for not knowing what was next. I was even scared for what people would think. To leave a well-recognised job to… well, I wasn't even sure at the time.

This wasn't merely a career shift; it was a shift to being led by my subconscious. The decision to start my own business, rooted in my passion for neuroscience, strategy and coaching, is all me and living in accordance with my authentic self. This realisation didn't just influence my career trajectory; it reshaped my entire life philosophy, around living the truest form of you.

LET'S BRAIN HACK: TUNING YOUR RADIO FREQUENCY

If you've never listened to your true self before, take a moment now and think about the parts in your life where something, a whisper, or a feeling in your body was telling you *'no'*, but you did it anyway.

What were those times?

_____

_____

_____

_____

What happened? Was it a good outcome, or a bad outcome?

_____

_____

_____

Now think about the parts or times in your life, where something, a whisper, a niggle or a feeling in your body was telling you a *'yes'*, and you did it.

Meet the Real You

What were those times?

_____

_____

_____

What happened? Was it a good outcome, or a bad outcome?

_____

_____

_____

Now think about the parts or times in your life, where something, a whisper, a niggle or a feeling in your body was telling you a *'yes'*, and you did not do it.

What were those times?

_____

_____

_____

_____

What happened? Was it a good outcome, or a bad outcome?

_____

_____

_____

What have you learnt from this exercise?

Have there been consistencies in those niggles, feelings, whispers in how they appear?

_____

_____

Let's now increase the dial and your understanding of your own subconscious self even further and create your own *'yes/no'* radio frequency.

Find a quiet space, take a deep breath, and clear your thoughts. This exercise will help you become more aware of how your body reacts to different types of statements, tuning into your subconscious reactions.

Step 1: General False Statements
Write down the following phrases that are clearly not true:

- We live on the sun.
- The ocean is red.
- Grass is purple.
- Rocks are soft.

Now, say these phrases out loud and observe how your body reacts.

Questions to Consider:
- Do you feel a constriction in your chest?
- Is there a tightness in your throat?
- Do you stumble over the words?
- Is your pitch low?
- What other physical sensations do you notice?
- Can you identify any other physical reactions, such as changes in your breathing or heart rate?
- How does your mind react? Do you feel confusion or disbelief?

Write down how your body instinctively reacts to statements that are fundamentally incorrect.

_____

_____

_____

_____

Step 2: General True Statements
Next, I want you to repeat the following accurate statements, noticing the difference in your physical response:
- We live on planet Earth.
- The sky is blue.
- Fire is hot.
- Humans breathe oxygen.

Say these a few times if needed. Pay attention to the sensations in your body and how much more natural these truths feel compared to the falsehoods.

Questions to Consider:
- Do you feel more relaxed and at ease?
- Is your breathing smoother and deeper?
- Is your pitch higher, lighter?
- How does your overall energy change?
- What other physical reactions do you notice, such as warmth or a sense of grounding?

How does your body react to these true statements? Write down your observations.

_____

_____

_____

_____

Step 3: Personalised False Statements

Write down and say the following false statements out loud:

- My name is <insert untrue name>
- I am <insert untrue gender alignment>
- I live in <insert false place of where you live>
- <insert any other silly, untrue statement>

Questions to Consider:

- How does your body react to these personal false statements? Do you notice physical reactions such as constriction, tightness, or discomfort?
- Are there any specific physical sensations that stand out with these personalised falsehoods?
- How does your mind process these false statements?
- Is there an immediate sense of disbelief, resistance, or confusion?

_____

_____

_____

Step 4: Personalised Affirm Statements

Write down and say the following true statements out loud:

- My name is <insert your name>
- I am <insert the gender you identify with>

- I live in <insert location you live in>
- <Insert any other true statements about yourself>

Questions to Consider:
- How does your body react to these true statements? Do you feel a sense of ease, relaxation, or warmth?
- Are there any specific physical sensations that stand out with these personalised truths?
- How does your mind process these true statements? Is there a sense of affirmation, comfort, or clarity?

_____

_____

_____

How did you go? Could you recognise the subtleties of the different statements?

You now have an inner beacon ready to help guide you through life. Use it to start to guide your life.

Meet the Real You

Key highlights to meet the real you

True alignment occurs when your inner truth and the life you lead are in harmony. This alignment between your conscious and subconscious selves allows you to make choices that reflect your deepest desires, values, and passions, leading to a life filled with purpose and fulfilment.

Western society often prioritises logical thinking over intuition, causing many to lose touch with their true selves. Reconnecting with your intuition and subconscious wisdom requires tuning out external pressures and focusing on your inner voice.

Start by listening to the whispers of your body and mind, paying attention to how different situations and decisions make you feel. Trust your intuition and make decisions that align with your true self, leading to a more intentional and fulfilling life.

CHAPTER 9

Vision Creates Clarity

As you unfurl yourself, unwind all the years of masks, personas, and adjusting yourself to your true self, it's now time to uplevel and create an awesome and amazing life around you. This is done based on you, your alignment with yourself, and creating whatever you see in your 'mind's eye'.

We are talking about goals… but not the normal verbiage around 'SMART' goals. On the internet, a single search on the term 'SMART goals' brings up 669,000,000 articles. Let me put that into words, Six hundred and sixty-nine million articles at the time that I wrote this. SMART goals are so widely discussed, referenced and applied throughout the world, particularly in business that this book is not another one of those books that leans on the 'SMART' goals concept. Yes, they do have their place, and I do use them in the appropriate settings, but from a personal perspective, I cannot stand that term. To really create a life full of richness and amazingness, I find them not inspiring enough, not meaty enough, and the concept of them keeps you confined in a little box.

I prefer a more holistic, flexible, and inspired approach to goal setting. One that has feeling, emotion and aligns with the complexity and richness of life itself. An approach that aligns with the brain's natural processes, unlocking the impossibilities. An approach that helps you get clear and creates clarity for you and your life, and moves you forward in ways that you cannot even comprehend. This is about redefining your whole game and creating your ultimate life vision!

Creating Your Ultimate Life Vision

Have you ever sat down and asked yourself, *'What do I actually want in life?'*

So, what do you want? When I ask this question, I often get many blank stares. You see, it's a simple question that many of us never stop to think about for ourselves. We overlook what we want in our lives as we get lost in the hustle and bustle of daily living.

Let's start breaking down this question further to help you be able to answer it. Imagine for a moment, that you are creating the very best day ever for yourself.

- What would you do?
- How would you feel?
- What activities would you find yourself doing?

Vision Creates Clarity

Spend a moment now to think about the answers to these questions. Go even further and spend a few minutes to picture it vividly in your mind. Now, let's stretch this vision further.

If you knew you had exactly five years left in your life:

- How would you spend it?
- What experiences would you want for yourself?
- How would you want to feel every day?

Yes, these questions and your answers might be big. But by spending time on these questions and the answers that they provide, they have the power to truly transform your life into what brings you joy and fulfilment.

True transformation lies in creating a life vision. A life vision has the power to transform your life and everything around you. A life vision enables you to create anything and everything you desire. It empowers you to create a life aligned to your true self. It creates clarity for you now and guides you through the minutia of the day to day and enables each day to be the building blocks of your best, fulfilling, amazing, and awesome inspiring life. It enables you to have excitement, motivation, and sets a path knowing exactly where you're heading and why. Not only that, but the brain, and more importantly, your subconscious is specifically primed to support you, and your vision.

Think back to the days of our ancestors, when survival depended on the ability to hunt for food. That goal — 'finding food' was a goal that the brain supported through what's known as the Reticular Activation System (RAS), a network in the brain that helps you focus on and achieve your goals. This same system is exactly what your brain uses to support you achieving your vision.

Another example of the RAS in action is when you've just bought a new car. A nice shiny new red car. Suddenly, you start seeing red cars everywhere. This is not a coincidence, it's your RAS at work now seeing all the red cars. The RAS acts as a filter for the vast amount of information your brain processes every second, allowing you to focus on what is most important to you. This means that when you create a clear and compelling life vision, your RAS will naturally help you notice opportunities, resources, and connections that align with your goals.

Now, back to vision setting. In setting your vision, I challenge you to set the biggest, boldest, most amazing things that you can imagine. Why? Because the most amazing things happen when you dare to dream big. When you set your sights on something that may seem beyond your current reach, you stretch your mind, your capabilities, and your potential in ways that small, safe goals simply cannot.

Big visions create excitement. Big ultimate life visions will push you out of your comfort zone. By aiming high, you will create a blueprint for your subconscious to follow. Every step you take, every decision you make, becomes aligned with that grand vision, propelling you forward even when the path isn't clear. It creates a life that excites, challenges and truly fulfils you.

MY JOURNEY

I have always been a very driven, motivated and determined person. If there was something that I wanted, or could see myself doing, I would just go for it and achieve it through hard work and persistence. When it came to visions and the concept of visions, I always had loose visions – these were mostly singular and to be honest, a result of the current life circumstances. Some of those being:

- Jump through uni – tick.
- The jobs opportunities available and potential career pathways available to a recent graduate, not that inspiring, let's go get a PhD to create new opportunities and pathways – tick.
- Uh oh, being in science after several years, not quite the life I was looking for – let's go get a job in 'business' and learn all about 'business' – tick.
- Without great luck on investing in shares and wanting to jump into property investing, our first house doubled as our first investment – tick.
- Build a property portfolio off the back of our first investment – tick.
- Change careers as I outgrew one, and dive into the next – tick.
- Complete the largest local area engagement nationally to rejuvenate a region - tick.

And so on and so on.

So, if you look at my achievements, you might wonder how could a broad ultimate life vision for myself, uplift and transform my life, when I have already achieved a lot?

Enter COVID.

As with everyone, COVID completely uprooted, and changed all routines and everything I knew. It was through this time of working out new routines that I not only reimagined my routines, but more specifically how I wanted to live my life, and what I wanted to have achieved in my life. It was as simple as sitting down with a blank sheet of paper in front of me, realising that I could create anything in my life that I wrote down on that paper.

It was a simple start, as I had never deliberately and so specifically thought about my desires and aspirations before from a holistic sense, having previously let myself be guided by the opportunities that unfurled as I skipped through life. And that approach is certainly ok, and worked until that point, but what more could a deliberate approach achieve?

I initially focused on three pillars: nourishing my mind, body, and soul, and drew a circle, cut into thirds. I asked myself what a life of fulfilment looked like. I envisioned that work and life for me as transformative, inspirational, catalysts for change, lots of creativity, growth, and value to me and who I was serving.

Vision Creates Clarity

Seeing these words on paper made me realise I needed to look inward to myself, for my work and life to embody these ideals. To truly grow and dig deep, I embarked on a renewed path of self-development. Each week, I dedicated hours to reading books, listening to podcasts, and attending virtual forums. This was also a part of my vision.

Having worked for the previous 15 years in Neuroscience, and self-development, I had learned a lot about myself and how I wanted to live. But it was this process that allowed me to learn more about myself and ask the deep questions I had never considered before.

After three months, I had made significant progress on realising everything that I had wanted to achieve on my vision board and felt ready to delve deeper into my desires and yearnings. This led to the next iteration of my vision board. During this process, I recognised the lingering clutter in my life and shifted my focus to clearing it away.

I asked myself crucial questions in the upgrade and development of my next vision board: What is serving me well right now? What is not serving me?

Answering these questions led me to make a bold decision—I let go of 18 months of hard work in one of my side hustles. I exited a company I had helped build from the ground up. It was a difficult decision, but it felt right when aligned with my vision board. Other achievements that were brought about from my vision board included:

- I started exercising again.
- I changed my food habits.
- I left the security of paid work to start my own business.
- I even paid off my property portfolio at the time!

The funny thing is that as I was leaving work, to jump into 'retirement'. One of my staff said, 'I'm not surprised. You said in your first week here that your next step in the next 5-6 years would be retiring!' Words that I spoke six years earlier, without memory, had come to pass, exactly as I had said them.

This is the power of a having a vision. And for me, having a vision board has been nothing short of transformative for me. What I thought, and wrote, gave me clarity on what I wanted with my life, and within weeks, I was finding myself on the path to these new hopes and dreams.

Writing out my life bucket-list of experiences, achievements, feelings, wants, desires, sharing it with my partner, got us focused, understanding each other deeply. But also enabled us to set some clear objectives for our next 90 days, year, ten years, and life.

One of those is what you are reading right now.

LET'S BRAIN HACK: CREATING YOUR VISION

Often when people write out their life vision, they find this task to be difficult. There is so much that can go into creating your vision, that this itself could be an entire book. But as a brain hack, I have deliberately kept it simple, to get you started, and enable you to create the same vision and changes in your life.

Creating Your Life Bucket List
- Write the numbers 1-50 on a blank piece of paper.
- Allow yourself the freedom to dream without restrictions. Write everything you want in life, no matter how big or small, realistic or fantastical.
- Use the prompts and questions below to help fill out all everything that you want in life if you get stuck.
    - Write all the experiences you want to have. Consider everything from adventurous activities like skydiving or scuba diving to simple experiences like watching a sunrise on a secluded beach. Think about cultural experiences, food adventures and personal milestones.
    - Write the things that you've always wanted to try but never did. What are the new skills that you want to learn? Perhaps it's learning a musical instrument, writing a book, or starting a new hobby.
    - List the places that you want to visit. Think about the cities, countries, natural wonders, and hidden gems around the world. Imagine the adventures

that you want to embark on, and the cultural experiences you want to immerse yourself in.
- o Who do you want to meet? This could include reconnecting with old friends, making new ones, or even meeting influential people who inspire you.

Look at all facets of your life – work, career, business, family, health, fitness, relationships, travel, and more and think about the impact that you want to have on others and the world, and any legacy you want to create.

As you fill in your life bucket list, dream big—think beyond impossibility, and let your imagination run wild. Envision scenarios that may seem far-fetched, but truly excite you.

Creating Your Life Vision
Now – let's get down to the nitty gritty and let's get creative!

Get yourself a blank piece of paper and choose your mode! Mind maps, drawings, paper cuttings, free-range writing, lipstick on the mirror… whatever creative means that resonate with you.

- Looking at your list, break it down to what do want to achieve over the next ten years, five years and 12 months.
- Once done – get granular, ask yourself – what do you want to have achieved over the next year?
- And then let yourself play in creativity to create your vision.

- It could be you write out, it is xxx date, and I have ... (finish the sentence).
- Or you get busy drawing, mind mapping or whatever else floats you.
- Articulate within your vision, how you want to be living your life. Describe your ideal daily routine, the type of environment you want to be in, and the lifestyle that would bring you the most joy and satisfaction.
- Articulate your feelings that you want to experience regularly. Consider emotions like joy, peace, excitement, love, fulfilment. Think about the activities or situations that will elicit these emotions and add them to your vision.
- Put your vision in a spot that you can regularly see and refer to.

Review, Add and Update
- Sit down every three months.
- Add to your bucket-list (yes – it's ok if you go over 50!).
- Review and add to your vision.

As you get into a rhythm, and achieve super-amazing stuff, push your boundaries for what is possible. Keep going. Within a few iterations, you will have found that you have up levelled your life.

Key highlights for vision creates clarity

Crafting a life vision goes beyond traditional goal setting. It's about understanding your true desires and creating a holistic, flexible vision that aligns with your inner self. This vision provides clarity, direction, and motivation, helping you build a fulfilling life.

The brain's Reticular Activation System (RAS) supports goal achievement by focusing on relevant information. When you dream big and set ambitious goals, your brain is primed to help you reach them.

Regularly reflecting on what truly matters to you helps prioritise your deepest yearnings and aspirations. Asking yourself questions about what you want in life, how you want to feel, and what experiences you crave, guides you towards a meaningful and aligned life.

CHAPTER 10

Expand your Possibilities

So, you have all the pieces in place. You've completed the hacks to get you to now. You've gotten clear on who you really are, and you've opened your mind to what you want in life, the experiences that you want, the life that you want to lead, and you've created a super amazing vision.

Let's really push the boundaries now, with a few pointed questions.

- Are all things in your life going well?
- As in everything?
- Are there any areas in your life that you are ignoring?

Without knowing it, have you been putting upper limits on parts of your life or parts of your success and happiness? Could this be that because perhaps, unconsciously, you believe that you don't deserve success and happiness across all areas of your life? Perhaps, you have put a subconscious ceiling for how much success, love, and abundance you believe you deserve across all areas of your life?

Uh oh.

What's that little niggle that's just started at the back of your mind?

- Maybe, you're much fitter now.
- Maybe your relationship with your partner is incredibly strong, or perhaps you're in a new relationship.
- Maybe you've changed careers, moved houses, or accomplished something you once thought impossible.

Well done.

But as we know, our brains have safety mechanisms that prevent us from stepping too far out of our comfort zones. Yes, you may be going extremely well in one part or a couple parts of your life. By working through this book now, more and more good stuff is happening in your life. Great! But are there parts of your life, where you might be upper limiting yourself?

Stop and think about all aspects of your life, relationships, friendships, career, personal life, health, fitness. And as you scan each area of your life ask yourself the following questions:

- Are you subconsciously sabotaging yourself in an area while you're going well in another area?
- Are there moments when you feel you don't deserve your success or happiness?

Expand your Possibilities

- Are you putting a self-sabotaging ceiling in any aspects of your life?

If you have said yes to any of these questions, that's ok. Acknowledge these feelings and then challenge them.

- What would happen if you truly believed you deserved all the good things that come your way?
- What would happen if there were no limits to what is possible?

Breaking Through Your Boundaries

When you first start asking yourself what you wanted for your life, and what you could achieve in your life, you might only think of some simple basics. Your vision may have been quite simple. As in achieve one or two things. Especially if you've never thought this way before. But as you start to achieve each item, you have grown, and through this experience, you naturally find yourself being able to imagine more and think more creatively. This is natural.

The brain likes to keep us safe and small; it's its way of ensuring that we don't get hurt. It's also its way of moving along the same record player grooves. Because to learn, and expand our possibilities requires energy – we are literally forging a brand new neuronal path.

What would happen if we push those boundaries that naturally occur with life experiences further and faster? How much more enriched and fulfilled could our lives become? Think about what you believe is possible for you right now, over the next week. A possible habit change, start of something new, research into a new endeavour.

What could be possible for you in 12 months?

Maybe you've got a new job or are planning a holiday, but let's think longer and bigger.

Perhaps imagine looking out five years into the future. Imagine if everything in your life changed beyond your wildest dreams. In five years, ten years, 20 years, anything is possible. It's such a long time to be able to dream big. Now, what if we condensed that time? What would it look like if all of what you thought was possible in five years, occurred within 12 months? You may not think that it's possible, but it certainly is possible.

You can make it possible by starting to push the boundaries of what you think is possible. Instead of aiming for incremental changes, what would radical transformations look like to you? What if you could double your income? What if you could create a thriving, successful business? What if you could achieve peak physical health? What if your personal relationships could be deeply fulfilling and supportive? Yes – all of that can happen in 12 months.

Yes – you can shortcut the time it takes to achieve your vision, but you can also increase the magnitude of your vision. I want you to extend and expand your vision even further than what you think is possible. If there's any resistance – identify it.

Push past the limits you've set for yourself and embrace the possibility that you can achieve more than you ever dreamed. As you continuously understand your current boundaries, and push

Expand your Possibilities

on those boundaries to expand and imagine and create new experiences, you're rewiring your brain to accommodate a broader conception of what's possible for you.

Expanding your possibilities is not just about achieving goals; it's about evolving into the person capable of living that envisioned life. As a child, we thought big and dreamed big without limits. As we grew, we often lost touch with those grand visions, and only thought about what's possible. It's time to reconnect with that childlike wonder and imagination and expand out your possibilities now. It's now time to think big again, and dream big, without limits.

MY JOURNEY

I often imagine going back to 15-year-old Simone, sitting in the library, pondering away her life in the library – as to what career I would choose, and what I might achieve. Fast forward 25 years, I would've had a great time telling my 15-year-old self that I would get a PhD in neuroscience with two of the world's leading researchers in mental health, and that I've had eight careers, including starting two businesses, and I'd been the architect and facilitator of the nation's largest local engagement, catalysing the rejuvenation of the area that I live in. I would've also said that I had not one, but two gorgeous and beautiful children, and helped so many live just as amazing and inspiring lives.

For my 15-year-old self, to have heard all of that, I would've been blown away, slightly scared (ok – who am I kidding, more like freaking out). My 15-year-old self would've run a mile thinking, how is any of that possible? How am I even capable of doing any of that? You see with the limited life experience that I had, all of that would be completely inconceivable to my 15-year-old self.

But all of this is possible, as I have lived and experienced it. It is easy to understand what's possible by looking back on your life and seeing what you have achieved, and then imagining going back to tell the younger version of yourself.

To be able to propel yourself to a future that has not existed, with even further possibility than what I have already achieved, and growth in identifying possibilities – that is the trick. To do this, I now regularly sit down and ask myself, what is possible. This book is a product of that. The someday, I'll write a book. However, now that I've started writing, my possibility has now expanded from writing this one book to now, four. Inconceivable before I put pen to paper on that very first word.

Here are some of the other possibilities that I have dreamed up for myself. All of it is possible to come to life.

- Working in my business ten hours a week?
- Retiring by the age of 40?
- Or push the possibilities further, retiring my partner in the next five years?
- Travel plans?
- Creating a popular podcast?

Expand your Possibilities

In pushing my boundaries even further, I've dreamed up crazy silly ideas. This includes being invited onto Richard Branson's Island, owning my own private island, launch a global charity, live off the grid, become a space tourist, invent a high-sought after revolutionary product, become a venture capitalist, live with a remote tribe and learning their ways, host a global summit, have a butler to clean my house, dye my hair the colour of the rainbow.

It doesn't mean that I must achieve every single one on the list, but it's about imagining what could be possible. And when I really like one – then I will certainly go for it. Hello rainbow hair! And yes, you can steal some of these for your own 'expand the possibility list' and push your limits further.

LET'S BRAIN HACK: EXPAND YOUR POSSIBILITIES

Now, it's your turn to break free from limitations and dream beyond your current reality. Expanding your possibilities is about opening your mind to the endless potential that lies within and around you.

Here's how you can start:

Step 1: Set a Weekly Alarm
Commit to expanding your possibilities by setting a weekly alarm. Go ahead now, set your alarm. This will serve as a reminder to take time out of your busy schedule to focus on dreaming big and envisioning your future without constraints.

Step 2: Brainstorm the Wildest Ideas
Write out the craziest, most outlandish things you could do. Don't censor yourself—let your imagination run wild. The goal is to push beyond what you think is possible. If you have trouble imagining, start by borrowing some ideas from my list above, or below.

Imagine: What if you could travel to space? What if you could start a new career that you're passionate about? What if you could live in a different country every year?

Steal Ideas: Owning a private jet, building an eco-friendly mansion, or create a global arts festival.

Expand your Possibilities

Think Big: Dream about creating a groundbreaking product, establishing a zero-waste community, or running marathons on all seven continents.

Keep adding to your list every week, allowing it to grow as you gain new insights and inspiration. Remember to have fun!

Step 3: Review and Choose
After a few sessions, look at your list. Choose which ideas excite you the most and feel aligned with your true desires and values. Choose a few that you'd like to focus on and start planning how to make them a reality.

Remember, the only limits are those you set for yourself. So go ahead, let your imagination soar, and have fun hacking your possibilities!

Key highlights to expand your possibilities

Recognise areas in your life where you might be subconsciously placing upper limits on your success, happiness, or abundance. Challenge self-imposed boundaries and explore what could happen if you truly believed you deserved all the good things coming your way.

Envision radical transformations instead of incremental change. By continuously understanding and expanding your boundaries, you can rewire your brain to accommodate a broader conception of what's possible.

As adults, we often lose touch with the grand visions that we had as children. Reconnect with that childlike wonder and imagination to think big and dream without limits.

CHAPTER 11

Transforming Lives With Lollipops

Every moment in our life has the potential to be life changing - not just for ourselves, but for anyone we meet or encounter on a passing basis. It is the everyday interactions, random encounters and words that hold the incredible potential to alter the course of a person's life in profound ways.

How is this possible?

One of my favourite TED talks is Drew Dudley's talk on 'Lollipop Moments': Drew Dudley: Everyday leadership | TED Talk. Sitting and watching Drew's TED talk many years ago was a Lollipop Moment for me. This short 5-minute video has changed my outlook, intent, and in ways the lives of every single person I have encountered since.

'Lollipop Moments' are those seemingly insignificant gestures, everyday activities, or acts of kindness that can often (without us realising) profoundly change another person's life. These are the moments where our actions, no matter how small, hit someone else at their core. These moments potentially alter their perspective, or boost their confidence, or inspire them to pursue their dreams.

The magic of lollipop moments is that they leave a lasting impression that ripples outwards, affecting not only the recipient but also everyone they interact with now and in their own life paths. Think of the butterfly effect, cascading out across the world.

You have great power to make a significant difference in the lives of people, your community, and the world. With you knowing the full impact of your thoughts, your actions, your words on others; you too can consciously create lollipop moments for those around you.

Opportunities to Create Lollipop Moments

Opportunities to create lollipop moments exist every single day. It's as simple as being present in the moment, showing kindness, and looking for opportunities to support and uplift others. By focusing on the positive impact you can have on others, you also find that in the process, your own life becomes richer, deeper, and more fulfilling.

Think about how you might be able to incorporate small acts of kindness every day, such as holding the door open, helping someone carry their groceries, or paying for a stranger's coffee. Find the space in your day to offer sincere compliments and words of encouragement to people. Recognise others' efforts and achievements, no matter how small they may seem.

Sometimes, just being there to listen can be incredibly powerful. Offer your time and attention to someone who needs to talk. Express your gratitude and appreciation for the people in your life. A simple thank you or a note of appreciation can go a long way.

You can create lollipop moments just by setting the intent that today could be the day where you change a person's life. By approaching each day with this mindset, you open the door for experiences not yet imaginable.

MY JOURNEY

Lollipop moments are the moments that I strive to create every day. In my coaching practice, I set myself the intention to create lollipop moments every coaching session that I have. When I present and facilitate workshops, I strive to create unique moments that leave people wondering. And when I meet people, I want to make them feel special.

For myself, I have received many lollipop moments in my life. In fact, my whole life has been a series of lollipop moments – those small, yet profoundly impactful gestures from others that have changed my life in ways I could never have predicted.

The Job Advertisement
Several years ago, I was at a crossroads in my career. The role I was in was a contract role, and I hadn't yet received an extension to that role. My substantive was one that I had grown out of and had no desire to return to. At that very crossroads, I had a lollipop moment, I saw a job advertisement for a senior role in strategy. Initially, I dismissed applying for the role, as I hadn't had any experience in Strategy at the time, and believing I lacked over 50% of the required skill set.

A colleague who knew me and my background well, insisted that I apply. She understood the type of work I would enjoy, better than myself at the time and recognised the transferable skills I possessed that would work well in a role in Strategy.

If not for her small nudge, I wouldn't have applied for the role. Her lollipop moment was having the belief in me. This propelled me to take a chance, which ultimately opened doors to some of the most fantastic opportunities and led me to where I am today.

Discovering My Unique Value
Initially, when I opened my business and started coaching, I was struggling to identify what was uniquely special about me to market myself effectively. During a meeting with another coach, she said, 'I know a lot of coaches, Simone, but I don't know any coach with a PhD in Neuroscience. You can market that.' While I did initially dismiss this insight, she insisted a second time, which made me take heed of my unique proposition.

This insight was a game-changer for me. It highlighted a distinctive aspect of my background that I had overlooked, helping me to position myself more effectively in the market. That simple, yet powerful statement gave me the confidence to embrace my unique qualifications and leverage them to build my brand. And here we are today.

Lollipop Moments with My Partner
Often in the proximity of our everyday life, I have received numerous lollipop moments from my partner. For example, sometimes he would pass job advertisements my way when I wasn't quite ready to look for new opportunities myself. His subtle nudges were a reminder that he saw potential in me, even when I was hesitant.

Another significant moment was when we've bought our houses to live in, simply by passing a 'for sale' sign when we weren't even looking. These spontaneous decisions, guided by a sense of opportunity and adventure, have shaped our lives in unexpected and wonderful ways.

LET'S BRAIN HACK: CREATING YOUR OWN LOLLIPOP MOMENTS

Understanding Your Lollipop Moments

Begin by reflecting on your own experiences. Think about moments in your life where a seemingly small action like a simple act of kindness, a word of encouragement, or a listening ear made a profound difference for you. These are your lollipop moments that you have received.

Write them down. Which specific actions or words changed your life? How did they make you feel? What was the outcome?

_____

_____

_____

_____

_____

_____

_____

Reflect on how these moments changed your perspective or changed the direction of your life.

If possible, reach out to thank the person who gave you that lollipop moment. Let them know how their action impacted you. Expressing gratitude not only honours the giver but also reinforces the importance of these moments in your own mind. I have also found that doing this, creates lollipop moments to the original giver.

Create Your Own Lollipop Moments with Others
Now that you've identified and reflected on the lollipop moments in your life, it's time to create them for others.

Each day, consciously set the intention to make a positive difference in someone's life. Remind yourself that every interaction holds the potential to be impactful.

Engage fully in your interactions. Listen attentively, respond thoughtfully, and show genuine interest in the people around you. Being present makes others feel valued and heard.

Reflect on the lollipop moments you created. You may even create a log like the following:

Your Lollipop Moments Log

Date: _____

Description of the Moment: _____

Impact on You/Other Person: _____

Reflection/Gratitude: _____

Use this log to document your daily lollipop moments, reflecting on the impact and expressing gratitude where appropriate. This practice will help you stay mindful of the power of small acts of kindness and their potential to create lasting positive change.

Key highlights for creating your lollipops

Everyday interactions and small acts of kindness – lollipop moments can profoundly impact another person's life. These moments can create a ripple effect of positive change.

Incorporate simple acts of kindness into your day, such as offering sincere compliments, helping someone with their groceries, or simply being there to listen.

Approach each day with the mindset, that today could be the day that you change someone's life.

CHAPTER 12

Let's Play

Cast your mind back to your childhood. Can you remember how happy you were, getting lost in your moments of play? Time would seemingly fly by, and all you had done was immerse yourself in the joy of play. Those were the moments when you felt truly alive, free from worries, and completely engaged in the present.

I love watching children now. Nothing is more important than the activity they are engaged in. They are immersed in that activity, with wonder and joy. This could be climbing over rocks. Playing with water, or bubbles, or pretend houses with toys. It could be brushing your pet's hair and 'styling' them. Or building amazing cities, planes, cars, or islands, with blocks, boxes, blankets or anything that is around. Everything as a child is play. From eating their food, to going to bed, to learning new skills, to interacting.

Ultimate Brain Hacks

Let's see how much you play, by asking yourself the following questions:

- As an adult, do you still play?
- How often do you play as an adult?
- What activities do you consider play?
- When was the last time you simply had fun?

For many of us, play is a forgotten luxury. The demands of work, family, and other responsibilities often push play to the bottom of our priority list. Or it's not even on our list. We tell ourselves that play is for children, that we are too busy or that it's not productive. Yet, play is just as important to us as adults as it is for children.

Play is just as important to us as adults as it is for children.

- Play keeps us young.
- Play helps us to imagine.
- Play brings a sense of lightness and fun.
- Play reconnects us with our inner child.
- Play reminds us of the joy and wonder we experienced as children.
- Play releases endorphins—our body's natural feel-good chemicals.
- Play provides an escape from the pressures of daily life, offering a space where we can relax and recharge.
- Play allows us to express ourselves freely and creatively.

At our core, we are inherently creative beings. Every single one of us is creative. If you do not see yourself as creative, let's reconnect you back to your creativity, and play is a natural outlet for this. When we play, we reduce our stress, we live in the moment, we experiment, and we explore new ideas. Most of all, we have fun.

We are fun beings, and we need more joy and laughter in our lives. Play creates moments of laughter and joy. Laughter, as they say, is the best medicine—it strengthens the way that we breathe, our immune system, our mental health, and improves our relationships.

With so many benefits, play needs to become a priority in your life. Embrace the power of play and watch as it transforms your life in wonderful ways.

MY JOURNEY

I first came across the concept of play and creativity several years ago. Yes, I was loving life, loving what I did, but a very serious 'professional' person working in the corporate world, not yet awakened to the true magic of life, or my true authentic self.

When the concept of play was first presented to me in a course, I thought *'humph'*. Yes, I'm being honest. *'Humph'*. I thought to myself, *'What type of a goal it that? What value would that give to a person? And besides I don't play… I mean, really?'*

My initial reaction was dismissive because like many adults, I had long ago relegated play to the back cobwebs of my mind, many, many years ago, in childhood. The idea of integrating play into my life seemed to me frivolous and unproductive. I was caught up in the demands of work, responsibilities, and the pursuit of more serious goals. Play felt like a luxury I couldn't afford, something that had no place in the practical, goal-oriented world of adulthood.

Everything changed with the birth of my daughter. Suddenly, play re-entered my life in the most natural and wonderful way. And I found myself more and more leaning into play. The seed of play having been planted earlier with this course that I had taken years before. For me, play today can range from jumping on the trampoline, chasing chickens, to throwing paper shredding into the air.

These simple, spontaneous activities have brought out a joy that I hadn't experienced in years. Watching my daughter's unrestrained delight and engagement with the world around her made me realise how much I had been missing.

Play creates pure joy in a moment. It is an escape from the daily grind, a chance to reconnect with my inner child, and an opportunity to see the world through a lens of wonder and possibility.

My journey into the world of play has transformed my perspective on life. If you find yourself dismissing the idea of play and creativity, allow yourself a moment to rediscover the joy and wonder that play can bring.

LET'S BRAIN HACK: LET'S PLAY

Schedule Your Play
Just as you schedule meetings and appointments, look at your calendar and make time for play in your calendar. It could be a weekly game night with friends, a daily walk in the park, or a weekend hobby. Treat playtime as an essential part of your routine, not as an optional activity. Go on and schedule it in now.

Work Out Your Play
What activities could be play for you? What sparks your creativity? Write them down.

_____

_____

_____

_____

Think about the activities that you enjoyed as a child or the ones that you find fun now.

This could be anything from painting, drawing, and writing, to gardening, cooking, or playing a musical instrument. Try sports, dance, yoga, or any physical activity that you enjoy.

Introduce fun rituals into your routine, such as making funny faces in the mirror or creating playful nicknames for household items. If you have children, join them in their play. Let their imagination and enthusiasm inspire you. Look at ways to create jokes or have fun in the moment. It could be mixing up your words to create new paradigms or adding colour to your wardrobe.

Bring laughter into your daily life. Watch a comedy show, read a funny book, or spend time with friends who make you laugh. Embrace spontaneity. Allow yourself to be spontaneous and open to unexpected moments of play. Be willing to say yes to activities that may seem silly or unproductive at first glance.

Key Highlights for let's play

Play as an adult is essential to our joy and happiness. It reconnects us to the wonder that we experienced as children.

Play can be scheduled, or it can be spontaneous. Look for moments of play in everyday life.

CHAPTER 13

Your Life Transformed

As you near the end of this book, the last brain hack is one of the most powerful and transformative. Reflection. Now it is time to reflect.

- Reflect on what you have learned.
- Reflect on your courage to look at yourself deeply.
- Reflect on how your life has transformed.

Reflection is one of the most powerful tools for self-awareness, growth, insight and understanding. Reflection is about asking yourself the right questions and creating new insights with your answers. If you sit on 'the balcony of your life' and ask yourself some querying questions about your day, week or month, you can create life-changing insights. Reflection can be done within any timeframe, daily, weekly, monthly, quarterly or yearly.

Ultimate Brain Hacks

The insights that you create from a short investment of time can pay dividends now and for future you. Some of the biggest insights for myself have come from the process of reflection. It's as simple as asking yourself some questions and collecting the answers and insights that you have.

Now it's time for you to reflect on your reading of this book.

It's now time to go back to your first intent and look at your notes from Chapter 1 and answer the following question.

Have you achieved your original intent? Yes – how? Or No – why not?

_____

_____

_____

_____

I want you to take some time to reflect on everything you've learned throughout this book. Do not skip to the end – just so that you can say you've finished another book. Take the time to sit down and actively reflect. Consider the insights that have resonated with you the most. Write them down and answer the following question.

Your Life Transformed

What have you learned from reading this book?

_____

_____

_____

_____

Well done.

Now think about the changes you've made in your life because of reading this book and answer the following questions.

What life changes have you made because of this book?

_____

_____

_____

_____

_____

_____

_____

How have these actions and changes impacted you and those around you?

_____

_____

_____

_____

Well done.

This act of reflection will help solidify your new knowledge and ensure it becomes a lasting part of your life.

Work out ways to implement reflection in your life. It could be as simple as daily/weekly/monthly/yearly wins, and challenges. And from those challenges, what have you learned about yourself? A simple reflection process can pay dividends to you in insight. So go ahead, pop some reflection time in your calendar.

My Invitation to You

Although I may not know you personally, I care deeply about your journey and your growth. You picked up this book for a reason, and I hope that it has served you well. I would love to hear about the changes you've experienced and the impact that this book, or more importantly - the insights that you have had while working through this book have had on your life.

Your Life Transformed

This is a genuine offer. I read and respond to every email that I receive. Your stories inspire me. Yes – I do a daggy fist-pump for every story, every win that I hear from the work that I do.

I wrote this book with the very clear intent to help you, the reader, and I care deeply about how you have grown, how you have changed, how you have become awakened from this book.

I also want to celebrate you. Celebrate you for coming this far. Celebrate you as you genuinely now know what you want in life. Celebrate you for how amazing you are and how you are living the most amazing, wonderful uplifting, magical life.

Life is a beautiful journey, and I want that you get to experience the same clarity, and journey for yourself.

I now invite you to reach out and share your journey with me. I am ready to fist-pump you and all your amazingness.

Here is my email: info@afreshapproach.com.au

Please feel free to write to me about your experiences, your growth, and the ways that this book has influenced you. I really look forward to hearing from you and celebrating with you.

So, go on – let me know how your life has changed. And celebrate you.

- Your story matters.
- You matter.

Ultimate Brain Hacks

As we close, remember that this is not the end of your journey—it's only the beginning. Your path to growth and self-discovery will continue, and I encourage you to embrace it fully. Self-discovery is a never-ending game, and as you pass through life, you learn more and more about yourself, and the wonderful experiences that you can create, and the feelings to be felt.

As we sign off, I want to say keep creating in your life, stay curious, embrace the endless possibilities that lie ahead and be magical.

Simone

References & Resources

The following resources have been referred to throughout this book:

"The ideal road not taken: The self-discrepancies involved in people's most enduring regrets" by Davidai, Shai and Gilovich 2018

Lollipop Moments TEDx Toronto, Drew Dudley 2010

Spark Joy: An Illustrated Master Class on the Art of Organizing and Tidying Up, by Marie Kondo, 2012

The Myth of Normal, by Gabor Mate 2022

The following resources are what I read and am inspired by:

The Big Leap, by Gay Henricks 2009

Breath, by James Nestor 2020

Untamed, by Glennon Doyle, 2020

About the Author

Simone Boer uses a unique blend of neuroscience, strategy and coaching to ignite crazy and transformative change in individuals and organisations. With a PhD in Neuroscience and over 20 years of experience in human behaviour, Simone has navigated through eight diverse careers, showcasing her belief in limitless personal and professional growth.

Known for her vibrant approach and ever-changing hair, Simone uses 'brain hacks' to help people overcome self-imposed limits and achieve unprecedented success. Simone has received numerous accolades, including Life Coach of the Year, 2023 and Transformational Coach of the Year 2023 and 2024.

Her strategic expertise has been pivotal in initiatives like the 'Clever and Creative' 30-year community vision for Greater Geelong, engaging 16,000 residents and reaching 750,000 people nationally.

Beyond her professional achievements, Simone is a devoted mother to two wonderful little people, whom she adores, loves, and cherishes. She is passionate about authentic living and career alignment, empowering clients to achieve goals they never thought possible. Simone loves indoor plants, staying fit and healthy, and infusing her life with creativity and joy.

You can contact Simone at: info@afreshapproach.com.au
Or jump online: www.afreshapproach.com.au

HAVE SIMONE COME AND SPEAK TO YOUR AUDIENCE!

Dr Simone BOER

Dr. Simone Boer leverages the power of neuroscience and strategy to drive transformative change in individuals and organisations. With a PhD in Neuroscience and over 20 years of experience in human behaviour, Simone has navigated through eight diverse careers, reflecting her belief in limitless personal and professional growth. Known for her vibrant approach and ever-changing hair, Simone uses innovative 'brain hacks' to help people overcome self-imposed limits and achieve unprecedented success.

Simone has been recognised with numerous accolades, including Life Coach of the Year 2022/2023 and Transformational Coach of the Year 2023/2024.

Simone's keynotes and workshops inspires and challenges participants to show up confidently, authentically and foster environments where they can lead with confidence and integrity.

Simone is dedicated to inspiring large-scale change in both individuals and organisations. Her goal is to empower individuals to believe in their capabilities, achieve the extraordinary, and feel deeply connected to their work.

Speaker and training topics include (but not limited to):

Ultimate Wealth Mindset Formula
- Transform Your Mindset for growth and success
- Understand Different Property Investment Strategies
- Your Retirement Game Plan to achieve financial freedom

Build high-performance teams
- Learn how to build a foundation of trust
- Implement techniques to ensure team members are committed to goals, to drive collective success
- Authority Branding to position yourself as a leading authority

Other topics include:

Ultimate Brain Hacks: 30 Brain Hacks to implement now to better your life and business

Set your vision for success (catering to both individual and organisations)

 info@afreshapproach.com.au   www.afreshapproach.com.au

Are you ready to uplevel your mindset and your life with 1:1 personal coaching with Simone?

Notes

www.ingramcontent.com/pod-product-compliance
Lightning Source LLC
Chambersburg PA
CBHW030301100526
44590CB00012B/480

ULTIMATE BRAIN HACKS

Unlock Your Mind. Return to Your Authentic Self. Transform Your Life.

Simone Boer, PhD

First published by Ultimate World Publishing 2024
Copyright © 2024 Simone Boer

ISBN

Paperback: 978-1-923255-71-5
Ebook: 978-1-923255-72-2

Simone Boer has asserted her rights under the Copyright, Designs and Patents Act 1988 to be identified as the author of this work. The information in this book is based on the author's experiences and opinions. The publisher specifically disclaims responsibility for any adverse consequences which may result from use of the information contained herein. Permission to use information has been sought by the author. Any breaches will be rectified in further editions of the book.

All rights reserved. No part of this publication may be reproduced, stored in or introduced into a retrieval system, or transmitted in any form, or by any means (electronic, mechanical, photocopying, recording or otherwise) without the prior written permission of the author. Any person who does any unauthorised act in relation to this publication may be liable to criminal prosecution and civil claims for damages. Enquiries should be made through the publisher.

Cover design: Aaron De Wit
Brain photo: Pexels.com by Amel Uzunovic under Pexels License
Featured illustrations: Khushmeen Sidhu and Aaron De Wit under License
Layout and typesetting: Ultimate World Publishing
Editor: Vanessa McKay

Ultimate World Publishing
Diamond Creek,
Victoria Australia 3089
www.writeabook.com.au

Testimonials

'An absolute game-changer! This book is packed with amazing insights and actionable steps that truly help you up level your life like no other. A must-read for anyone looking to unlock their full potential!'
Allyson Brown, PhD, Director, everheal

'Simone is amazing at what she does as a coach through her knowledge of neuroscience! She can help you achieve your wildest dreams with great hacks to build your confidence, set your goals and then go after them.'
Carlo Lowdon, Director, e3 Products

'Working with Simone's Brain Hacks has been life changing. I was initially a bit sceptical, however the real power comes from the tools and techniques to change your mindset. They are tools for life, and it changes how you look at the world. Having felt stuck career-wise for many years and not knowing what to do next, I have been able to make good progress on finding my next path. I have achieved so much in such a short amount of time.'
Daniel Appleby

'You can draw from Simone's vast life/professional experience, brain hacks and motivational resources to improve your life. Some of the highlights involve hypnotherapy, goal setting, action plan prep, and getting to know myself on a deeper level with shadow values. I would recommend Simone's Brain Hacks to anyone who is 'stuck' in life or have lofty goals but need a helping hand reaching them.'
Mathew Kirk